The 1812 Catalogue
of the
Library of Congress

A Facsimile

Introduction by Robert A. Rutland
Indexes by Lynda Corey Claassen

LIBRARY OF CONGRESS
WASHINGTON 1982

Library of Congress Cataloging in Publication Data

Library of Congress
  The 1812 catalogue of the Library of Congress.

  Reprint. Originally published: Catalogue of the
books, maps, and charts belonging to the library
established in the Capitol at the City of Washington
for the two houses of Congress, to which are annexed
the statutes and bye-laws relating to that institution. Washington City : printed by R. C. Weightman,
1812.
  Includes indexes.
  Supt. of Docs. no.: LC 1.2:C28/8/1812
  1. Library of Congress—Catalogs. I. Rutland,
Robert Allen, 1922–   . II. Claassen, Lynda C.
Z881.W3238A17   1982   018′.1′0973   81-607118
  ISBN 0-8444-0382-2   AACR2

For sale by the Information Office, Library of Congress,
Washington, D.C. 20540.

Table of Contents

iii

Foreword

This volume offers us a unique glimpse of the intellectual vistas from Capitol Hill during the founding decades of the Republic. One of its most remarkable revelations is that in those days a respectable, cosmopolitan, and comprehensive library could be shelved on the walls of two rooms. Then, more than now, the contents of Congress's Library probably suggested the contents of the best informed congressional minds. Of course, it is not likely that any member of Congress read all or even most of the works listed here. But the range of subjects and the quality of the books are reliable clues to what members thought they ought to know, and how they hoped to secure their knowledge.

In those days, before any member had a staff, each member had to do his own digging, and here is where he dug. Few other nations can offer their citizens such a vivid museum of their own intellectual history, of the furnishings of minds who shaped their nation's earliest years. Here we have a reminder of the youth of our nation. By collecting and displaying these works together we can give Americans today an exhilarating vision of the culture, the cosmopolitanism and omnivorous curiosity of our early statesmen—in a country which most of the Western world still considered remote and semicivilized. We can see that they were as determined to "ransack the archives of ancient prudence" as to marshall the resources of their own "enlightened age." Their breadth of mind, their hunger for the lessons of nature, geography, and history, has inspired our representatives ever since, and still inspires our Library of Congress to follow their example in the modern mode.

Daniel J. Boorstin
The Librarian of Congress

v

Introduction

The city of Washington may have fewer monuments, archways, statues, and fountains than London, Paris, or Rome, but in one sense our national capital is far ahead of all others. The Library of Congress makes that difference. Eighteen million volumes stacked in the shadow of the Capitol may be more printed books than the British, French, and Italian national libraries hold *combined*. If this seems like American boasting, let it be recalled that when the rest of western civilization was well on its way—with ancient universities, royal galleries, and ducal libraries of vast extent—the United States was still struggling for a place in the family of nations.

In 1776 the odds against survival were high. The same men who fought the American Revolution were determined to see their early vision of a Union triumph, however, and by 1789 they had shaped a government that could offer life, liberty, and the pursuit of happiness to its four million citizens. Within a decade, the people's elected representatives made a commitment to maintain free government by drawing upon their common sense, love of freedom, and the stored knowledge of mankind. Amply blessed with the first two ingredients, they made their gesture for the third in Philadelphia during the spring of 1800 as they hurried toward adjournment at the temporary capital while preparing to move to new, permanent quarters along the lower Potomac.

As the packing and crating took place, the small collection of books Congress then possessed went aboard a freight ship at the Philadelphia docks. Although over ten thousand citizens had taken up residence in the new capital at Washington, there were discouraging reports of muddy streets which became pigsties during wet weather.

The shops were poorly stocked, so rumors ran, and the social life was skimpy. Congress sought to solve several problems with one bill. "An Act to make provision for the removal and accommodation of the Government" contained a $10,000 appropriation for sidewalks and $5,000 "for the purchase of such books as may be necessary for the use of Congress . . . and for fitting up a suitable apartment for containing them and for placing them therein." Months would pass before the Library of Congress could allow a senator or representative to borrow a book or read a newspaper. For a time, the sidewalks had priority.

Despite congressional attention to such exigencies, the gesture made by Congress in appropriating the $5,000 is a landmark in the intellectual life of the nation, for apart from the delays and crowded housing, the 1800 law signaled the fledgling republic's intention to put books as working tools in the hands of its legislative craftsmen. After a decade of experience under the Constitution, the congressmen realized that a perfect government was beyond their reach. What they sought was a workable republican model, and most lawmakers interested in a library for Congress had been present when the nation was born a generation earlier. There had been much experimentation and some failure. Many recalled that back in 1782, when the Revolution was almost over, Congress had tried to establish its own library and brought forth a splendid list of required books. Nothing came of that effort, except that it set men to thinking. Moreover, the young congressman who drafted the list of books—Delegate James Madison of Virginia—would be heard from again.

Why did books figure prominently in the congressmen's thinking? Remember that from President Adams (who signed the 1800 bill) on down through the ranks, these were men who had used histories, political treatises, and the works of Greek and Roman philosophers as ammunition in their assault upon the colonial ties with England in the 1760s and 1770s. Indeed, Jefferson relied on his traveling library when he drafted the Declaration of Independence, and Madison combed through scores of volumes on ancient republics when he prepared himself for the 1787 convention in Philadelphia. Beyond a doubt, the new nation was based on courage, sweat, blood, and knowledge. The private libraries at Braintree, Monticello, and Montpelier were as important as redoubts or palisades. Books did more to shatter the British hold on America than ten thousand muskets.

On July 1, 1782, Theodorick Bland, a member of the Virginia delegation serving with Madison and Jefferson, asked for the purchase of books "for the use of the United States in Congress assembled." No doubt the three had often been frustrated as they worked on committees and prepared legislation without the aid of books. The Library Company of Philadelphia and the private collections in the vicinity of Congress Hall, at Sixth and Chestnut Streets, must have helped—but there was a need for a well-stocked library close at hand. Madison was appointed chairman of the committee assigned the task of preparing "a list of books to be imported" for the congressmen's business, with his teacher from Princeton days—John Witherspoon—and New Englander John Lovell as colleagues. Finally ready early in 1783, Madison's list ran to 307 titles, probably over two thousand actual volumes, and the compilation reveals the sources of the ideas that influenced men of action during the Revolution. The books ranged from the intellectual bombshell of the eighteenth century—Diderot's *Encyclopédie*—to Nicolas del Techo's *Historiae Paraguaria*. It included all the English books used to brew the revolutionary ferment (Sidney, Harrington, Locke, Hume) and a goodly selection of similar works from continental authorities (Machiavelli, Montesquieu, Beccaria). Immensely practical, Madison's list had no room for belles lettres or anything that lacked utilitarian purposes.

But Congress was unable to act on Madison's recommendations. The national government never appropriated money for the book purchases because the treasury was empty, so when Madison left Congress the report was pigeonholed. Moreover, picking the place to keep the books would have caused problems. During the war the capital had moved at various times from Philadelphia to Lancaster and York in Pennsylvania, to Princeton, New Jersey, and to Annapolis and Baltimore in Maryland, in order to escape British entrapment. Philadelphia had been the first meeting site in 1774, but there was much dissatisfaction with William Penn's model city. During the summer there was always the threat of a devastating yellow fever epidemic. In winter the roads north and south were impassable and river ferries were frozen fast until the spring thaws.

A central location for the national capital was finally chosen in 1790, when the First Congress settled upon a site on the lower Potomac. Congressman Elbridge Gerry's attempt during the First Congress to create a congressional library for members' use died in a committee. A decade would pass before Congress took permanent residence on the knoll where Washington rode on horseback across what became Capitol Hill. There, as workmen swung beams and hauled blocks of granite into place, the congressmen from the growing republic (there were sixteen states in the Union by 1800) soon found that there were woeful inconveniences to be encountered in a wilderness. Only a smattering of books had been bought during the decade by the secretary of state and made available to Congress in its makeshift quarters. Vattel's *Law of Nations* and 242 other titles filled the shelves of the secretary's office—an obviously temporary arrangement. Once the legislators were settled in the newly christened city of Washington, a separate, well-lighted room would be needed.

Congress reconvened in its new quarters in November 1800, but the joint committee created that spring to buy books in response to that first appropriation of $5,000 had already acted. The library committee sifted through the requests and suggestions of senators and congressmen and ultimately chose the London firm of Cadell & Davies as agents for its purchases. Sen. William Bingham and Rep. Robert Waln compiled the list of books and dispatched it in June on a London-bound vessel. This was to be a working members' library, containing mainly references that a country lawyer might need if he moved into the complicated business of maritime or international law.

By the time the British booksellers filled the order, Jefferson was president and his ideas on frugality were in effect. Even though Cadell & Davies had sent the 740 volumes in trunks "rather than boxes, which after their arrival would have been of little or no value," Jefferson thought the Englishmen's £498 bill too high. Congress, to save money, ordered the trunks sold, and Jefferson wrote the American consul in London to bestir himself in search of bargains. Jefferson also instructed the consul to seek plain bindings and to avoid expensive folio editions when smaller volumes would serve congressmen as well as "pompous ones."

Perusing that first printed booklist,* Jefferson's eye must have fallen on the entry for volumes that cost a staggering £105—the *Parliamentary Debates* (104 volumes) and *Journals of the Lords and Commons* (102 volumes). Could

---

* A facsimile of this *First Booklist of the Library of Congress* is available from the Information Office, Library of Congress, Washington, D.C. 20540.

good republicans learn that much from the monarchical maneuverings of Whigs and Tories? Most of the books were general histories (fifty-nine titles), and one set was David Hume's *History of England* (eight volumes), which Jefferson had admired when a college student, before he decided the books offered a "perverted view" of the English constitution. And the book that Jefferson considered a republican antidote to Hume, John Baxter's *New and Impartial History of England*, was altogether missing from the list. A conspicuous set (sixty volumes) was *An Universal History, from the Earliest Account of Time . . . ,* compiled by George Sale and others between 1736 and 1745. Jefferson could not praise this work too highly, and in 1825 he still spoke of this set of volumes as a key acquisition for the new University of Virginia Library. "The ancient universal history should be on our shelves as a book of general reference, the most learned and most faithful perhaps that ever was written."** Also on Madison's 1783 list, this third edition of the work stood high in the opinion of most educated Americans as the authoritative chronicle of events from 4004 B.C. forward, following the Biblical calendar and beginning of course with Adam and Eve's trespasses. Little space was left for belles lettres—an outlay of only £7 10s. going for the much-admired *Spectator* and *Tatler* (with other familiar essays) in an eighteen-volume set.

After first being stored in an anteroom, the London purchases were combined with small collections (probably reference books) used by the House and Senate. All were brought together under one roof in 1802. The temporary chamber first used by the House as a meeting place was hastily converted into a joint library. Eighty-six feet long and thirty-five feet wide, with a thirty-six-foot

** Jefferson to [George Washington Lewis?], October 25, 1825, in *The Writings of Thomas Jefferson*, ed. Andrew A. Lipscomb (Washington: The Thomas Jefferson Memorial Association, 1904), 16: 124–5.

ceiling, the room had two rows of windows that admitted plenty of light. Rules for the Library of Congress were established to keep the doors open from 11:00 A.M. to 3:00 P.M., except on the Sabbath, and a member of Congress was to be allowed to remove only two books at any one time. A clause in pending legislation which created a Librarian of Congress and required frequent reports of expenditures also would have permitted cabinet officers, Supreme Court justices, and foreign ministers to use the Library; but crusty John Randolph pounced on this intrusion in the affairs of Congress and the bill which became law confined use to members of the House and Senate. One change in the operation of the Library was established by the 1802 law—a salary of two dollars per day was to be paid to the Librarian. Not much of a political plum, but still a welcome appointment for John Beckley, who took on the new duty along with his old post as clerk for the House.

Rarely has a president been as interested in what his congressional colleagues read as was Thomas Jefferson. Invited by a senator serving on the joint library committee (and thus reversing the direction of advice specified in the Constitution), Jefferson prepared a list of works he thought necessary "to the deliberations of the members as statesmen, and . . . omitted those desirable books, ancient and modern, which gentlemen generally have in their private libraries, but which cannot properly claim a place in a collection made merely for the purposes of reference." Like Madison, Jefferson was keen on books dealing with international law. "I have put down everything I know of worth possessing, because this is a branch of science often under the discussion of Congress, and the books written on it [are] not to be found in private libraries." Money for Jefferson's suggestions was soon forthcoming, for Beckley found $2,480.83 of the original appropriation unspent. Thus while Jefferson was dealing with obstreperous congressmen in his own party and trying to soothe the opposition, he still found the time to recommend titles for the Library of Congress.

Despite Jefferson's admonition, more money went into bindings than probably suited the president. When the artist Charles Willson Peale visited the refitted Library of Congress in 1804 in the company of other dignitaries, the guests tended to judge the books by their covers. "The Library is a spacious and handsome Room," Peale recorded in his diary, "and although lately organized, already contained a number of valuable books in the best taste of binding."

Meanwhile, the House reneged on its decision to keep the Library in a well-lighted, "suitable apartment." In 1805 the Library was moved to a former committee room that was in a bad state of repair, with loose floorboards and a leaky roof. The rules on borrowing had been relaxed, too, for on November 26, 1805, Beckley had to call on Secretary of State Madison to return six volumes of the *Annual Register*, "Grotius Puffendorf and Sir William Temple's *Works* . . . before the meeting of Congress" which was scheduled for the following week. Rank had its privileges, but Beckley wanted all the books back on the shelves before the members of Congress came to town.

Although the Library was now in cramped quarters, the Senate offered a new member for the joint committee who proved to be a fitting companion for the likes of Madison and Jefferson. Samuel Latham Mitchill, a New York physician who had served three terms in the House, was elected to the Senate and soon busied himself with Library business. A man of broad scientific interests, Dr. Mitchill was known to contemporaries as a "stalking library." He soon complained that the Library resources in literature and science were pitifully thin. There was also a dearth of "geographical illustrations," Mitchill told the Senate early in 1806, as he recommended that "steps be seasonably taken to furnish the library with such materials as will enable statesmen to be correct in their investigations, and, by a becoming display of erudition and research, give a higher dignity and brighter lustre to truth." Congress was persuaded. An annual appropriation of $1,000 was approved to strengthen the Library collection of books and maps.

During these seedling years the Library had a devoted friend in the White House but some enemies in the halls of Congress. Speaker Nathaniel Macon seems never to have consulted its shelves and was so frugal-minded he told a colleague he considered the Library a "useless expense" which Congress ought to abolish. Sen. William Plumer defended the cost, for he loved books and thought the Library was an oasis "in this desert-city." But even Plumer could be easily riled, and he became incensed when a popular book, full of scandal from Napoleon's court, was in constant circulation. "Such a currency has scandal," Plumer huffed, but he also noted that the Library stacks were expanding. By the end of 1806 the room, with a roof still leaking, housed nearly two thousand volumes.

In April 1807 Jefferson's long-time friend and confidant Beckley died, leaving the House clerkship and the head post at the Library vacant. Within days a swarm of applicants laid quiet siege on the White House, but Jefferson was in no hurry to name a replacement. He waited until the following November to appoint Patrick Magruder, a sometime student at Princeton who had turned to politics and served one term in the House before losing a re-election battle in 1806. Magruder also won Beckley's old place as clerk to the House, so Jefferson was following a precedent of his own making in naming Magruder to dual offices. During the Beckley and Magruder eras, it is fairly clear that the Librarian was a kind of custodian who was responsible for the office but who left the day-to-day business in the hands of subordinates. The actual selection of books remained a duty of the conscientious joint committee, which supervised purchases, asked for a new book catalogue, and late in 1807 paid a call on President Jefferson to discuss the state of the Library.

Senator Mitchill's joint committee prepared the report that led to publication of the 1808 rules and regulations with its details on openings and closings, lending rules, and fines. To discourage the tardy borrowers, fines were set according to the size of the book, with penalties of three dollars per day for folio editions, two dollars for quarto-sized books, and a dollar for smaller books. However, either the president of the Senate or the Speaker of the House was permitted to excuse all or part of the fine "for good cause." In the circumstances, the income from fines was a pittance. More important was the forty-page catalogue printed in 1808 to show a three-fold expansion of the Library in less than four years. Moreover, a "buy American" campaign had borne fruit as purchases were now being channeled to Boston, New York, and Philadelphia rather than to booksellers abroad. And a number of gifts found their way to the stacks as congressmen, eager to tell of products from their home districts, offered the Library locally printed essays, tracts, and sometimes a bound volume.

As the diary entries and letters from Plumer, Mitchill, and other members of Congress indicate, the legislators were not hard at work at all times—although the cultural delights of the new capital were few. Most congressmen lived in boardinghouses on Capitol Hill which took on the atmosphere of watered-down London clubs, with wives rarely in attendance. One of Mitchill's richest legacies is the hundreds of letters he wrote to his wife back in New York describing the comings and goings, the debates, and sometimes the intrigue taking place in Congress. The roads in Washington were dusty in summer, muddy in the fall, and frozen in winter, so that it took a hardy soul to seek exercise on horseback or even to ride down Pennsylvania Avenue across several wooden bridges to the distant White House. In such circumstances, the Library of Congress probably served members at times as a social gathering place, for it was open until 7:00 P.M. on the days when Congress was in session. The smaller books were the most popular and could be taken for only one week, which meant an increasing circulation for the few romantic novels, plays of Shakespeare, and similar books that made their first appearance late in Jefferson's second term. In fact, the Library must have been a refuge for certain congressmen with bookish habits who did not relish the card-playing, interminable conversations, and heavy drinking that took place in many boardinghouses after the Senate and House adjourned for the day.

An increasing number of congressmen deserted Capitol Hill after their official duty ended to return to their Georgetown lodgings. Senator Breckinridge noticed the exodus in 1804 and blamed it on the boardinghouse operators who "have raised their prices to such a pitch of extravagance, that a great number of members have taken Lodgings in George Town." Mitchill joined the crosstown lodgers as he complained of rising costs on Capitol Hill and noted that the company in Georgetown was far more agreeable. The pronounced split between the Federalist and Republican parties also had side effects in the members' social life. Federalist Simeon Baldwin, a representative from Connecticut, observed in 1803 that "the men of different parties do not associate intimately. Federalists live mostly by themselves, there are about 50 in both Houses, of these we have 13 at our own Table."

When Jefferson vacated the White House in 1809, the Republicans controlled Congress, had elected Madison as president (in 1808) with little difficulty, and seemed more firmly entrenched than ever. Actually, a number of congressional coalitions and factions honeycombed the party, but on the surface the administration of James Madison boded well for the tight-fisted Republicans. Pledged to eliminating the national debt, they continued to cut corners on defense spending despite the major war being waged in Europe, and taxes were cut bone-deep. Still Congress expanded the Library under the watchful eye of Mitchill, who had gone back to the House from the Senate but retained his place on the joint committee. Mitchill was probably the moving force behind the issuance of the 1812 catalogue of the nation's storehouse of printed knowledge which is reproduced here in facsimile.

Printed library catalogues were the only device then available for readers seeking a book. There were no card catalogues, there was no numerical or even alphabetical classification system, and the practice was the same in the great libraries in Rome and London—a printed catalogue described the holdings but an all-knowing clerk probably found the book scattered among the increasing number of folios or quartos.

A catalogue tells of more than growth, however. In the case of the 1812 Library catalogue, we can discern changing and expanding tastes. In addition, a considerable step forward was made in this catalogue by introducing the subject categories, beginning with "Sacred History" and proceeding to the unbound maps and charts. This innovation, along with the table of contents, gave members of Congress an opportunity to survey the books at their disposal by simply turning to the section devoted to "Civil History" or "Natural History" or "Gazettes" (newspapers). This idea for improved service in the Library was an early step toward the Library of Congress classification system that has now gained worldwide acceptance.

A perusal of the 1812 catalogue also tells us that the United States was still engaged in a cultural struggle for its nationhood. Notice that most of the books were printed abroad—the majority in London.* The capital of the British empire was also the center of the printed word for those who counted English as their mother tongue. Select a page or two at random, and notice that only occasionally will there be a smattering of books published elsewhere. Indeed, page 27 lists the most books (148) and all except six were printed in London. Already the signs of change were visible, however, and within another generation the trend had been reversed as American printers moved into book publishing with the same zeal which marked other fields of commercial enterprise. In 1812, a war year, the young nation was straining for both military success and a cultural break with England. This catalogue shows that the Library which would be set to a British torch within two years time was mainly a collection of British books.

Apart from that irony of war, the catalogue gives us a clear idea of what Americans thought important in 1812. The Library of Congress combined all the characteristics of a law office, coffeehouse reading room, scholar's nook, and cleric's study. Where Jefferson in 1802 had told the chairman of the joint committee "that books of entertainment" were "not within the scope of it," there now appeared a full section on "poetry, drama, works of fiction, wit, &c." The president's businesslike list had not included the poems of Ossian, but by 1812 a Philadelphia edition of the works of "the greatest poet who had ever

---

* An index to places of publication follows the catalogue facsimile.

existed" (Jefferson's own claim) was nestled between Philip Freneau's works and Bloomfield's *Farmer's Boy*. How many congressmen shared Jefferson's enthusiasm for Ossian is uncertain, for here was a great literary hoax in the making (and finally exposed late in the nineteenth century). What catches the eye on this list is the forty-nine volumes of works by British poets and the twenty-five volumes of Mrs. Elizabeth Inchbald's *British Theater*—a treat for congressmen who liked plays and found the playbill fare sparse to nonexistent in the "city" of Washington. These small books (along with Mrs. Inchbald's collection of *Farces*) contained a stream of plays that first hit the boards at the Theatre Royal, Covent Garden, and other London playhouses.

Washington had no public library, of course, so a congressman either bought or borrowed his reading. If he was looking for an evening with his head pleasantly buried in a book, he also could have chosen from Rabelais, Cervantes, Shakespeare, or Washington Irving's *Knickerbocker's History of New York*. The choices were limited for, after all, this was the epitome of a reference library—a place that would be as useful to a legislator as the workbench for a cobbler.

The casual entry under "Miscellaneous Literature" of the sixty-two-volume set of the *Gentleman's Magazine* (from 1731 to 1787) would seem to be an exception to this rule. The title of this British literary clearinghouse makes it seem more appropriate for a club off London's Pall Mall than for a legislative reading room. But in fact this periodical was treasured by public men as the leading reporter of parliamentary debates for several generations—for a time thinly disguised as "Debates in the Senate of Lilliput" and finally, after 1771 (when the House of Commons gave up its battle to prevent publication of its speeches), a valuable source of what Whigs and Tories were saying during the critical years 1774–83.

When we recall that most of these books—nearly three thousand of them—became a British bonfire, there is an inevitable touch of sadness as we perceive the loss of treasures that would now bring spectacular bids at book auctions. An oil sheik's ransom would be required to reassemble a library containing such rarities as Boswell's *Journal of a Tour to the Hebrides*, Bartram's *Travels*, the original Fry-Jefferson map of Virginia, or the first edition of Thomas Hutchinson's *History of the Colony of Massachusetts-Bay*. Yet we know that all these treasures were not so regarded in 1812, for in that practical age the ledgers showed only that less then $15,000 had been spent in accumulating all these books for the lawmakers' use.

While we can lament the loss of 1814, we can also learn much from the information gleaned from the 1812 catalogue. Although prepared for the members of Congress, it carried a larger message. The people ruled, through their representatives, and those who served in Congress were to renew the foundations for their liberties. To some extent the congressmen were the grandchildren of the Enlightenment, looking to precedents as their guides while realizing that their home-grown republicanism and common sense had to be the ultimate criteria. The 1812 Library of Congress catalogue tells us that the Harvard-trained senator and the untutored representative from a frontier state drew from the same body of knowledge just as they shared the same national aspirations. Washington was no visionary "City on a Hill" but a busy place where liberty and the pursuit of happiness would be sought anew at each session of the Congress by men constantly mindful of their commitment to the learning symbolized by the printed words, as Jefferson insisted, "in neat but not splendid bindings."

The Library of Congress of today holds within a few hundred cubic feet of shelf space more books than this

1812 catalogue lists, but in our time we are pressed to maintain the fervor for learning so much in evidence then. "The use of words is to express ideas," Madison reminded his generation. The words and ideas of 1812 still speak to us, for the experiment in self-government which the history of the Library of Congress chronicles so well is an ongoing process. Thus the challenge remains.

ROBERT A. RUTLAND
Editor-in-Chief
The Papers of James Madison
University of Virginia

Selected Readings

Cole, John Y., ed. *For Congress and the Nation: A Chronological History of the Library of Congress.* Washington: Library of Congress, 1979.

———— *The Library of Congress in Perspective.* New York and London: R. R. Bowker Company, 1978.

Goodrum, Charles A. *The Library of Congress.* New York and Washington: Praeger Publishers, 1974.

Jefferson, Thomas. *The Writings of Thomas Jefferson.* Edited by Paul L. Ford. 10 vols. New York: G. P. Putnam's Sons, 1892–99.

Johnston, William D. *History of the Library of Congress.* Vol. 1. Washington: Government Printing Office, 1904.

Librarians of Congress, 1802–1974. Washington: Library of Congress, 1977.

Madison, James. *Papers of James Madison.* Edited by William T. Hutchinson and William M. E. Rachel (vol. 1–7) and Robert A. Rutland et al. (vols. 8–). Chicago: University of Chicago Press, 1962–77; Charlottesville: University Press of Virginia, 1978–.

Malone, Dumas. *Jefferson and His Time*. 6 vols. Boston: Little, Brown, 1948–81.

Mearns, David C. *The Story Up to Now: The Library of Congress, 1800–1946*. Washington: Government Printing Office, 1947.

Mugridge, Donald H. "A Shipment of Books." *Quarterly Journal of the Library of Congress* 8 (November 1950): 5–16.

The Facsimile

CATALOGUE

OF

THE BOOKS, MAPS AND CHARTS,

BELONGING TO

THE LIBRARY

ESTABLISHED

IN THE CAPITOL AT THE CITY OF WASHINGTON,

FOR THE

TWO HOUSES OF CONGRESS:

TO WHICH ARE ANNEXED

THE STATUTES AND BYE LAWS

RELATIVE

TO THAT INSTITUTION.

WASHINGTON CITY:

PRINTED BY ROGER C. WEIGHTMAN.

1812.

STATUTES.

AN ACT

Concerning the Library for the use of both Houses of Congress.

[Passed January 26, 1802.]

Sec. 1. *BE it enacted by the Senate and House of Representatives of the United States of America, in Congress assembled,* That the books and maps purchased by direction of the act of Congress, passed the twenty fourth of April, one thousand eight hundred, together with the books or libraries which have heretofore been kept separately by each house, shall be placed in the capitol, in the room which was occupied by the House of Representatives, during the last session of the sixth Congress.

Sec. 2. *And be it further enacted,* That the President of the Senate, and Speaker of the House of Representatives, for the time being, be, and they hereby are empowered to establish such regulations and restrictions in relation to the said library, as to them shall seem proper, and from time to time, to alter or amend the same: *Provided,* That no regulation shall be made repugnant to any provision contained in this act.

Sec. 3. *And be it further enacted,* That a librarian, to be appointed by the President of the United States solely, shall take charge of the said library, who, previous to his entering upon the duties of his office, shall give bond, payable to the United States, in such a sum, and with such security as the President of the Senate and Speaker of the House of Representatives, for the time being, may deem sufficient, for the safe keeping of such books, maps and furniture as may be confided to his care, and the faithful discharge of his trust, according to such regulations as may be, from time to time, established for the government of the said library; which said bond shall be deposited in the office of the Secretary of the Senate.

Sec. 4 *And be it further enacted* That no map shall be permitted to be taken out of the said library by any person; nor any book, except by the President and Vice-President of the United Sates, and Members of the Senate and House of Representatives, for the time being.

Sec 5 *And be it further enacted,* That the keeper of the said library shall receive for his services, a sum not exceeding two dollars per diem, for every day of necessary attendance; the amount whereof, together with the necessary expenses incident to the said library, after being ascertained by the President of the Senate and Speaker of the House of Representatives, for the time being, shall be paid out of the fund annually appropriated for the contingent expenses of both Houses of Congress.

Sec. 6. *And be it further enacted,* That the unexpended balance of the sum of five thousand dollars appropriated by the act of Congress aforesaid, for the purchase of books and maps for the use of the two Houses of Congress, together with such sums as may hereafter be appropriated to the same purpose, shall be laid out under the direction of a joint committee, to consist of three members of the Senate, and three members of the House of Representatives.

AN ACT

For the disposal of certain copies of the laws of the United States.

[Passed January 2, 1805.]

Sec. 1. *BE it enacted by the Senate and House of Representatives of the United States of America, in Congress assembled,* That three hundred copies of the laws of the United States, which have been procured by the Secretary of State, in obedience to the law passed for that purpose, and three hundred copies of the journals of Congress, which have been procured in pursuance of the resolution of the second of March, one thousand seven hundred and ninety nine, shall be placed in the library of Congress.

Sec. 2. *And be it further enacted,* That the Secretary of the Senate, for the time being, be, and he is hereby authorised to receive three hundred copies of the laws of the United States, out of the thousand copies reserved by law for the disposal of Congress, as soon as the same shall be printed after each session; which he shall cause to be placed in the library, and assorted respectively with the sets of copies mentioned in the first section of this act; excepting only, that at the close of the present session, which will complete the eighth Congress, and in like manner after each particular session in future, which shall complete a Congress, he shall cause the several copies, reserved by him as aforesaid, for all the sessions of each respective Congress, to be bound in one volume, making three hundred volumes for each Congress, as aforesaid; which he shall cause to be placed in the library, assorted with the respective sets of copies mentioned in the first section of this act. And the several copies of the laws and journals of Congress, mentioned in this act, shall not be taken out of the library, except by the President and Vice President of the United States, and members of the Senate and House of Representatives for the time being. And the expense of binding shall be paid, from time to time, out of the fund appropriated to defray the contingent expenses of both Houses of Congress.

Sec 3 *And be it further enacted,* That the President of the Senate and Speaker of the House of Representatives, for the time being, be, and they are hereby empowered to establish such regulations and restrictions in relation to the copies of the laws and journals of Congress, directed by this act to be placed in the library, as to them shall seem proper, and from time to time, to alter and amend the same: *Provided,* That no regulation nor restriction shall be valid, which is repugnant to the provisions contained in this act.

Sec. 4. *And be it further enacted*, That to make up the deficiency of the appropriation heretofore made, for the purchase of four hundred copies of the laws of the United States, the sum of eleven hundred and forty-four dollars be, and the same is hereby appropriated, payable out of any money in the Treasury, not otherwise appropriated.

AN ACT

Making a further appropriation for the support of a Library.

[Passed February 21, 1806.]

BE it enacted by the Senate and House of Representatives of the United States of America, in Congress assembled, That in addition to the unexpended balance of the former appropriation made to purchase books for the use of Congress, which is hereby revived and continued, there shall be appropriated the sum of one thousand dollars yearly, for the term of five years; to be paid out of any monies in the Treasury not otherwise appropriated, and expended under the direction of a joint committee, to consist of three members of the Senate, and three members of the House of Representatives, to be appointed every session of Congress, during the continuance of this appropriation.

AN ACT

In addition to an Act, entitled, " An Act concerning the Library for the use of both Houses of Congress."

[Passed May 1, 1810.]

BE it enacted by the Senate and House of Representatives of the United States of America, in Congress assembled, That the President of the Senate and Speaker of the House of Representatives, for the time being, be, and they are hereby authorised to grant the use of the books in the library of Congress to the Agent of the joint committee of Congress appointed in relation to the library, on the same terms, conditions and restrictions, as members of Congress are allowed to use said books, any thing contained in any former law to the contrary notwithstanding.

AN ACT

Making a further appropriation for the support of a Library.

[Passed December 6, 1811.]

BE it enacted by the Senate and House of Representatives of the United States of America, in Congress assembled, That in addition to the balance of the former appropriations made to purchase books for the use of Congress, there shall be appropriated the sum of one thousand dollars yearly for the term of five years; to be paid out of any monies in the Treasury not otherwise appropriated, and expended under the direction of a joint committee, to consist of three members of the Senate, and three members of the House of Representatives, to be appointed every session of Congress, during the continuance of this appropriation.

Concurrent Resolve in favor of the Judges of the Supreme Court.

[Passed March 2, 1812.]

RESOLVED by the Senate and House of Representatives of the United States of America, in Congress assembled, That the President of the Senate and the Speaker of the House of Representatives, for the time being, be, and they are hereby authorised, to grant the use of the books in the library of Congress, to the Judges of the Supreme Court of the United States, at the times and on the terms, conditions and restrictions, as members of Congress are allowed to use the said books.

Conformably to which Resolve, the President of the Senate and the Speaker of the House, did grant the privilege to the Judges, by a writing under their hands, and directed to the Librarian.

The joint committee, appointed by the two Houses of Congress, at the commencement of the second session of the twelfth Congress, in November, 1812, consists of the following members:

On the part of the Senate,

MICHAEL LEIB,
CHARLES TAIT, and
GEORGE W. CAMPBELL.

On the part of the House of Representatives,

SAMUEL L. MITCHILL,
ADAM SEYBERT, and
JAMES EMOTT.

CONTENTS.

———

CATALOGUE

OF

THE BOOKS, MAPS AND CHARTS,

BELONGING TO

THE LIBRARY OF CONGRESS.

SACRED HISTORY.

FOLIO.

No.   Vols

1   The Holy Bible.   Thompson and Small's edition.
      Philadelphia, 1798.   1

ECCLESIASTICAL HISTORY.

FOLIO.

2   Father Paul's History of the Council of Trent.
      Translated from the Italian, by Sir Nathaniel
      Brent.   With the life of the author, and the
      History of the Inquisition.   London, 1676.   **1**

OCTAVO.

33   Mosheim's Ecclesiastical History, Ancient and Mo-
      dern, from the birth of Christ, to the beginning
      of the present century.   Philadelphia, 1797.   6

CIVIL HISTORY, INCLUDING CHRONOLOGY, BIOGRAPHY, ANTIQUITIES, &c.

A.

FOLIO.

No.   Vols.

5   Appian's History of the Punick, Syrian, Parthian, Mithridatick, Illyrian, Spanish and Hannibalick Wars, and the Civil Wars of the Romans. London, printed, 1679.   1

QUARTO.

71   Arbuthnot's Tables of Ancient Coins, Weights, and Measures, explained in several dissertations. London, 1727.   1

OCTAVO.

89   Arrian's History of Alexander's Expedition, translated from the Greek, with notes, &c. By Mr. Rooke. London, 1729.   2

178   Adolphus' Biographical Memoirs of the French Revolution. London, 1799.   2

180   Anquetil's Universal History, exhibiting the Rise, Decline and Revolutions of the different nations of the world, from the creation to the present time; 2 sets. 9 vols. each. London, 1800.   18

283   Annales de la Petite-Russie; ou Histoire des Cosaques-Saporogues et des Cosaques de L'Ukraine, ou de la Petite Russie, depuis leur origine jusqu'à nos jours. Par Jean-Benoit Scherer. A Paris, 1788.   2

355   A General History of Connecticut, from its first settlement under George Fenwick, Esq. to its latest period of amity with Great Britain. By a gentleman of the province. London, 1781.   1

383   An Historical Review of the Constitution and Government of Pennsylvania, from its origin; 2 copies. London, 1759.   2

417   An Account of Louisiana, being an abstract of documents, in the offices of the Departments of State and of the Treasury; 3 copies.   3

DUODECIMO.

B.

FOLIO

No.   Vols.

335 Belgian Traveller (the) or a Picture of the Empire
      of Buonaparte, and his Federative Nations:
      being a tour through Holland, France and
      Switzerland, during the years 1804-5. 2 copies.
      Middletown, (Conn.) 1807.   2

374 Belknap's History of New-Hampshire; .compre-
      hending the events of one complete century
      from the discovery of the river Pascataqua.
      Philadelphia, 1784.   3

385 Bozman's History of Maryland, during the three
      first years after its settlement. Baltimore, 1811.   1

422 Barton's Views of the Origin of the Tribes and
      Nations of America. Philadelphia, 1798.   1

444 Belknap's American Biography; or an Historical
      Account of those persons who have been dis-
      tinguished in America, comprehending also a
      recital of the events connected with their lives
      and actions. Boston, 1794.   2

454 Burke's Account of the European Settlements in
      America. London, 1777.   2

471 Biographical Dictionary (a new and general) con-
      taining an historical and critical account of
      the lives and writings of the most eminent
      persons in every nation; from the earliest
      accounts of time to the present period. Lon-
      don, 1798.   15

DUODECIMO.

9 Bossuet's View of Universal History, from the
    beginning of the world to the empire of Char-
    lemagne. Translated from the French, by
    James Elphiston. London, 1778.   2

C.

FOLIO.

25 Clarendon's History of the Rebellion and Civil
     Wars of England, from the year 1641 to the
     year 1660. Oxford, 1704.   4

69 Collier's Historical Dictionary, or Miscellany of
     Sacred and Prophane History. London, 1701.   4

QUARTO.

23 Clavigero's History of Mexico, with plates and critical dissertations on the land, the animals, and inhabitants of Mexico. Translated from the Italian, by Charles Cullen. London, 1787. *See also No.* 425 *octavo,* 3 *vols. Philadelphia,* 1804.   2

54 Coxe's Memoirs of the Life and Administration of Sir Robert Walpole. London, 1798.   3

58 Clarke's Letters concerning the Spanish Nation; written at Madrid during the years 1760 and 61. London, 1763.   1

OCTAVO.

119 Coote's Continuation of Russell's Modern Europe; and a View of the Progress of Society, from the peace of Paris, in 1763, to the treaty of Amiens, in 1802. Philadelphia, 1811.   1

259 Coote's History of the Union of the Kingdoms of Great Britain and Ireland; with an Introductory Survey of Hibernian Affairs, traced from the times of Celtic colonization. London, 1802.   1

274 Catteau's General View of Sweden; containing an account of its constitution, religion, population, and form of government as established in 1772, &c. &c. Translated from the French. 2 copies. London, 1790.   2

281 Card's History of the Reign of Charlemagne, considered chiefly with reference to religion, laws, literature and manners. London, 1807.   1

282 Card's History of the Revolutions of Russia, to the Accession of Catharine the First; including a concise review of the manners and customs of the Sixteenth and Seventeenth centuries. London, 1803.   1

188 Chenier's Present State of the Empire of Morocco; its Animals, Products, Climate, &c. &c. The history of the dynasties since Edris, and the character, conduct and views, political and commercial, of the reigning Emperor. Translated from the French. London, 1788. 2 sets, 2 vols. each.   4

No.   Vols.

303 Coxe's Memoirs of the Life and Administration
     of Sir Robert Walpole, Earl of Orford,
     London, 1800.   3

306 Charnock's Biographical Memoirs of Lord Vis-
     count Nelson, with observations critical and
     explanatory. New York, 1806.   1

330 Campaigns of the Armies of France, in Prussia,
     Saxony and Poland, under the command of his
     Majesty the Emperor and King, in 1806 and
     1807: in which the great events of that memo-
     rable era, and the brilliant achievments of the
     generals, officers and soldiers, are recorded.
     Accompanied with biographical notices upon
     those who fell during that memorable cam-
     paign. Translated from the French by Samuel
     Mackay. 2 sets, 2 vols. each. Boston, 1808.   4

359 Collections of the Massachusetts Historical So-
     ciety. A periodical work, the first vol. printed
     in Boston 1792, the last in 1809.

398 Colden's History of the Five Indian Nations of
     Canada, with particular accounts of their man-
     ners, customs, laws, religion, &c. &c. London,
     1750.   1

420 Coxe's View of the United States of America, in
     a series of papers, written at various times be-
     tween the years 1787 and 1794. 2 copies, Phi-
     ladelphia, 1794.   2

504 Collections of the New York Historical Society,
     for the year 1809. Presented by the honora-
     ble Samuel L. Mitchill, in behalf of the Socie-
     ty. New York, 1811.   1

506 Collection of State Papers, relative to the war
     between Great Britain and France. From
     1791 to 1799. London.   8

639 Clarendon's Parliamentary Chronicle; containing
     the proceedings and debates of the Houses of
     Lords and Commons, during the years 1790,
     91, 92, and 1793. London   7

645 The Congressional Register, or history of the pro-
     ceedings and debates of the first House of Re-
     presentatives of the United States of America.
     By Thomas Lloyd. New York, 1790.   3

D.

FOLIO.

QUARTO.

OCTAVO.

DUODECIMO.

E.

QUARTO.

48   Edward's Civil and Commercial History of the British Colonies in the West Indies. London, 1794.   2

OCTAVO.

502   Esprit de L'Histoire Generale de L'Europe. Depuis l'an 476 jusqu'à la Paix de Westphalie. A Londres, 1783.   1

DUODECIMO.

39   Espriella's Letters from England. Translated from the Spanish. Second American edition. New York, 1808.   2

F.

OCTAVO.

101   Ferguson's History of the Progress and Termination of the Roman Republic. Edinburgh, 1799.   5
Froissart's Chronicle of England, France, Spain, and the adjoining countries; from the latter part of the reign of Edward the Second, to the coronation of Henry the Fourth. Translated from the French, by Thos. Johnes. London, 1808, with a quarto volume of plates.   12

319   Forbes (Sir William) Account of the Life and Writings of James Beattie, including many of his original letters. Philadelphia, 1806.   1

322   Fox's History of the Early Part of the Reign of James the Second. Philadelphia, 1808.   1

G.

QUARTO.

13   Gibbon's History of the Decline and Fall of the Roman Empire. London, 1789.   6

OCTAVO.

74   Gillies' History of Ancient Greece, its Colonies and Conquests; from the earliest accounts, till the division of the Macedonian empire in the east, including the history of literature, philosophy, and the fine arts. London, 1792.   4

No.   Vols.

131   Guicciardini's History of Italy, from the year 1490, to 1532. Translated from the Italian, by A. P. Goddard. London, 1753.   10

257   Gordon's History of Ireland, from the earliest account, to the union with Great Britain, in 1801. London, 1806.   2

293   Gillies' View of the Reign of Frederick the Second King of Prussia; with a parallel between that Prince and Philip the second, of Macedon. London, 1789.   1

324   Goldsmith's State of the French Republic, at the end of the year eight. Translated from the French of Hauterive. Dublin, 1801.   1

340   Grellman's Dissertation on the Gipseys, representing their customs and manners generally, with an historical inquiry concerning their origin and first appearance in Europe. Translated from the German. London, 1807.   1

412   Gordon's History of the Rise, Progress, and Establishment of the Independence of the United States of America; including an account of the late war; and of the thirteen colonies, from their origin, to that period. London, 1788.   4

II.

FOLIO.

3   Helvius' Historical and Chronological Theatre. London, 1787.   1

16   Herbert's (Lord) History of the Life and Reign of Henry the Eighth. London, 1672.   1

QUARTO.

3   Hampton's Translation of the General History of Polybius. London, 1777.   2

32   Hume's History of England, from the invasion of Julius Cæsar, to the Revolution in 1688. London, 1770.   8

50   Harte's Life of Gustavus Adolphus, King of Sweden; 2 sets, 2 vols. each. London, 1759.

66   Hardy's Memoirs of the Political and Private Life of James Caufield, Earl of Charlemont. London, 1810.   1

No.   Vols.

67. Histoire des Guerres et des Negociations que pré-
cédèrent le Traitié de Westphalie. Par le Père
Bougeant. A Paris, 1767.   3

OCTAVO.

86   Herodotus, (the general history of), translated
from the Greek, with notes, by Wm. Beloe.
London, 1791.   4

120   Henry's History of Great Britain, from the invasion
of it by the Romans under Julius Cæsar, till the
year 1547, written on a new plan. London,
1799.   12

234   Hume's History of England, from the invasion of
Julius Cæsar, to the revolution in 1688. London, 1792.   16

270   Hannibal, (the course of, over the Alps, ascertained). By J. Whitaker. London, 1794.   2

276   History of Poland, from its origin as a nation, to
the commencement of the year 1795. London,
1795.   1

358   Hutchinson's History of the Colony of Massachu-
sett's Bay, from the first settlement, in 1628,
until its incorporation with the colony of Ply-
mouth, province of Main, &c. by the charter of
William and Mary, in 1691. London, 1755.   1

370   Holme's American Annals, or a Chronological
History of America, from its discovery, in
1492, to 1806. Cambridge, 1805.   2

395   Heriot's History of Canada, from its first discovery;
comprehending an account of the original establishment of the colony of Louisiana. London, 1804.   1

430. Humboldt's Political Essay on the kingdom of
New Spain. Translated from the original
French, by John Black, with a separate volume
of maps, &c. New York, 1811.   3

434. Herrera's General History of the Vast Continent
and Islands of America, commonly called the
West Indies, from the first discovery thereof;
with the best account the people could give of
their antiquities. London, 1743.   6

DUODECIMO.

16   L'Histoire des Empereurs. A Paris, 1767.   2

I & J.
FOLIO.

OCTAVO.

K.
QUARTO.

443   Memoirs of William Sampson, including particu-
      lars of his adventures in various parts of Eu-
      rope, his confinement in the dungeons of the
      Inquisition in Lisbon, &c. &c. &c. New York,
      1807.   1

494   Mirabeau (le comté de) de la Monarchie Prus-
      sienne, sous Frédéric le Grand; contenant des
      recherches sur la situation actuelle des princi-
      pales contrées de l'Allemagne. A Londres,
      1788.   7

DUODECIMO.

2   Millot's Elements of the History of France; trans-
     lated from the French.   London, 1771.   3

6   Memoirs of the House of Brandenburg, from the
     earliest accounts to the death of Frederick the
     First, King of Prussia. By Frederick the Third,
     King of Prussia.   London, 1757.   2

42   Memoirs of Marmontel, written by himself, con-
     taing his literary and political life, and anec-
     dotes of the principal characters of the eigh-
     teenth century.   Philadelphia, 1807.   2

45   Morse's Compendious History of New England,
     designed for schools and private families.
     Charlestown, 1804.   1

60   Memoirs of Ninon de l'Enclos.   Translated from
     the French by Mrs. Griffith.   Philadelphia,
     1806.   1

N.

FOLIO.

2   Newton's (Sir Isaac) Chronology of Ancient King-
     doms amended.   To which is prefixed a short
     chronicle from the first memory of things in
     Europe, to the conquest of Persia by Alexan-
     der the Great.   London, 1728.   1

OCTAVO.

148 Noble's Memoirs of the Protectoral House of
     Cromwell; deduced from an early period, and
     continued down to the present time; and also
     the families allied to, or descended from them:
     collected from original papers and records:
     embellished with engravings, &c.   London,
     1787.   2

No.   Vols.

268   Naylor's History of Helvetia, containing the rise
        and progress of the Federative Republics, to
        the middle of the fifteenth century. London,
        1801.   2

342   Necker's Historical Review of his own Adminis-
        tration. Translated from the French. London,
        1791.   1

372   Neal's History of New England, containing an
        impartial account of the civil and ecclesiastical
        affairs of the country to the year 1700. Lon-
        don, 1747.   2

P.
QUARTO.

60   Present State of Peru; from original and authentic
        documents, chiefly written and compiled in the
        Peruvian capital. Embellished by twenty en-
        gravings of costumes, &c. London, 1805.   1

OCTAVO.

78   Pausanias' Description of Greece. Illustrated
        with maps, views, &c. London, 1794.   3

106   Plutarch's Lives, translated from the Greek, with
        notes critical and historical, and a new life of
        Plutarch. By John and William Langhorne,
        London, 1792.   6

199   Puffendorf's Introduction to the History of the
        Principal States of Europe. London 1764.   2

201   Parliamentary History of England; or an account
        of all the most remarkable transactions in par-
        liament, from the earliest times to the restora-
        tion of Charles the Second. London, 1757.   20

399   Present State of Nova Scotia, with a brief account
        of Canada, and the British Islands on the coast
        of North America. Edinburgh, 1787.   1

252   Plowden's Historical Review of the State of Ire-
        land, from the invasion of that country under
        Henry the Second, to its union with Great
        Britain on the first of January 1801. Philadel-
        phia, 1805.   5

320   Peters (History of the Rev. Hugh) arch-intendant
        of the prerogative court of Doctors Commons.
        By the Rev. Samuel Peters. New-York, 1807.   1

525   Parliamentary Debates from the year 1620 to the
        year 1800 inclusive.   104

DUODECIMO.

S.

QUARTO.

OCTAVO.

384   Salmon's Chronological Historian, containing a
        regular account of all material transactions and
        occurrences, ecclesiastical, civil and military,
        relating to English affairs, from the invasion
        of the Romans, to the fourteenth year of
        George the second. London, 1747.   2

381   Smith's History of the Province of New York,
        from the first discovery. London, 1777.   1

382   Smith's History of the Colony of New Jersey, con-
        taining an account of its first settlement, pro-
        gressive improvements, &c. &c. Burlington,
        N. J. 1765.   1

387   Stith's History of the Discovery and Settlement of
        Virginia. Williamsburg, 1747.   1

505   Stuart's Historical Dissertations on the Antiquity
        of the English constitution. London, 1770.   1

DUODECIMO.

46   Stiles's History of Three of the Judges of Charles
        the First, Major General Whalley, Major Ge-
        neral Goffe, and Colonel Dixwell; who at the
        restoration in 1660 fled to America, and were
        secreted in Massachusetts and Connecticut.
        Hartford, 1794.   1

47   Steele's Naval Chronologist of the Late War, from
        its commencement in 1793, to its conclusion in
        1801; with a description of Lord Nelson's vic-
        tory off Cape Trafalgar, in 1805, and a plan of
        that engagement. London, 1806.   1

T.

FOLIO.

29   Thurloe's collection of State Papers, containing au-
        thentic memorials of the English affairs, from
        1638, to the restoration of Charles the Second;
        with the life of Mr. Thurloe, by T. Birch.
        London, 1742.   7

73   Townshend's Collections of the Proceedings of the
        Four Last Parliaments of Queen Elizabeth.
        London, 1680.   1

QUARTO.

1   Thucydides' History of the Peloponnesian War.
        Translated from the Greek, by William Smith.
        London, 1753.   2

U.

OCTAVO.

1 Universal History, Ancient and Modern, from
the earliest accounts to the present time, compiled from original authors, &c. London, 1784. 60

V.

OCTAVO.

159 Voltaire's History of the Age of Louis the Four-
teenth; to which is added an abstract of the
age of Louis the Fifteenth. Translated by R.
Griffith. London, 1779.   2

161 Voltaire's History of Charles the Twelfth King of
Sweden. Translated by W. S. Kenrick. To
which is added the life of Peter the Great. By
J. Johnson. London, 1710.   1

326 Vaness' Life of Napoleon Buonaparte; containing every authentic particular by which his ex-
traordinary character has been formed; with a
concise history of the events that have occa-
sioned his unparallelled elevation, and a philosophical review of his manners and policy as a
soldier, a statesman, and a sovereign: including
memoirs and original anecdotes of the Imperial
Family, and the most celebrated characters
that have appeared in France during the Revolution. Illustrated with portraits. Philadelphia, 1809.   4

341 Vendée (an Historical Sketch of the Civil War in
the) from its origin to the peace concluded at
La Jaunaie. Translated from the French of
P Y. I. Berthre de Bourniseaux. Paris, printed at the English press, 1802.   1

DUODECIMO.

1 Volney's Lectures on History, delivered in the
Normal school of Paris. Philadelphia, 1801. 1

13 Vertot's Revolutions de Portugal. A Paris, 1758. 1

W.

FOLIO.

67 Wood's Athenæ Oxonienses, or an Exact History of
all the Writers and Bishops who have been educated in the University of Oxford. London,
1721.   2

OCTAVO.

No.   Vols.

151 Watson's History of the Reign of Philip the Second
     King of Spain. 2 sets, 3 vols. each. London,
     1794.   6

157 Watson's History of the Reign of Philip the Third
     King of Spain. London, 1793.   2

323 Wilson's History of the British Expedition to
     Egypt; to which is subjoined, a sketch of the
     present state of that country and its means of
     defence. With maps, &c. Philadelphia, 1803.   1

345 Williams's (Helen Maria) Political and Confidential
     Correspondence of Lewis the Sixteenth; with
     observations on each letter. London, 1803.   3

377 Williams's Natural and Civil History of Vermont.
     2 copies. Walpole, New Hampshire, 1794.   2

379 Same work, the second edition, corrected and much
     enlarged. Burlington, Vt. 1809.   2

396 Wynne's General History of the British Empire in
     America: containing an historical, political, and
     commercial view of the English settlements;
     including all the countries in North-America,
     and the West-Indies, ceded by the peace of
     Paris London, 1770.   2

405 Washington's Monuments of Patriotism; being a
     collection of the most interesting documents
     connected with the military command, and ci-
     vil administration of the American hero and
     patriot. Philadelphia, 1802.   1

409 Warren's (Mrs.) History of the Rise, Progress and
     Termination of the American Revolution. Pre-
     sented by the Authoress. Boston, 1805.   3

490 Whiston's Translation of the Works of Flavius Jo-
     sephus, the learned and authentic Jewish his-
     torian and celebrated warrior. London, 1806.
     See also No. 80, *Duodecimo,* 6 *vols.*   4

DUODECIMO.

7 Wendeborn's View of England towards the Close of
   the Eighteenth Century. Translated from the
   German, by the author himself. Dublin, 1791.   2

64 Watts's edition of the Life of William Pitt; with
    biographical notices of his principal friends.
    Philadelphia, 1806.

X.

OCTAVO.

GEOGRAPHY AND TOPOGRAPHY, VOYAGES AND TRAVELS.

A.

QUARTO.

OCTAVO.

DUODECIMO.

C.

FOLIO.

QUARTO.

No·   Volsł

22 Coxe's Account of the Russian Discoveries between Asia and America: to which are added,
the conquest of Siberia, and the history of the
transactions and commerce between Russia
and China. London, 1780.   1

23 Coxe's Travels into Poland, Russia, Sweden and
Denmark. Interspersed with historical rela-
tions and political inquiries. Illustrated with
charts and engravings. London, 1784.   3

45 Chuchard's Geographical, Historical and Political
Description of the Empire of Germany, Hol-
land, Switzerland, Prussia, &c. &c. With a
gazetteer, and statistical tables. London,
1800.   1

OCTAVO.

7   Cruttwell's Universal Gazetteer, containing a description of all the empires, kingdoms, states,
&c. in the known world. London, 1798.   3

49 Carey's American Pocket Atlas; containing nine-
teen maps, and a brief description of each state.
Philadelphia, 1801.   1

50 Carver's Travels through the Interior Parts of
North America, in the years 1766, 67 and 68.   1

51 Charlevoix's Voyage to North America; contain-
ing the geographical description and natural
History of that country, particularly Canada.
Together with an account of the customs, cha-
racters, manners, &c. of the original inhabitants.
Translated from the French. London, 1761.   2

34 Clarke's Travel's in Various Countries of Europe,
Asia and Africa. Philadelphia, 1811.   1

D.

FOLIO.

1   Geographie Ancienne abrégé.   Par M. D'Anville.
A Paris, 1769.   1

2   Atlas de D'Anville.   1

4   Dunn's New Atlas of the Mundane System.
London, 1800.   1

Desbarre's Atlantic Neptune.   London.   1

OCTAVO.

14 D'Anville's Compendium of Ancient Geography.
Translated from the French. London, 1791.   2

E.

QUARTO.

DUODECIMO.

F.

OCTAVO.

No.   Vols.
108 Fêtes et Courtisanes de la Grèce. Supplement aux
     Voyages d'Anacharsis et d'Antenor. A Paris,
     1803.   4

G.
FOLIO.

6 Atlas to Guthrie's System of Geography. 3
   copies.   3

QUARTO.

1 Guthrie's System of Modern Geography; or, a
   Geographical, Historical and Commercial
   Grammar;, and present state of the several
   kingdoms of the world. Sixth edition. Lon-
   don, 1795.   1
2 Same work. Fifth edition. London, 1792.   1
3 Same work. First American edition. Philadel-
   phia, 1794.   2

OCTAVO.

12 Gazetteer of Scotland, containing a particular des-
    cription of that kingdom.   Edinburgh, 1806.   1
42 Grandpre's Voyage in the Indian Ocean and to
    Bengal, in the years 1789 and 1790: containing
    an account of the Sechelles Islands and Trinco-
    male.   To which is added a voyage in the Red
    Sea; including a description of Mocha, and of
    the trade of the Arabs of Yemen.   Translated
    from the French.   London, 1803.   2

DUODECIMO.

2 Gazetteer of France.   London, 1793.   3

H.
FOLIO.

Heather's Marine Atlas, or Seaman's Complete
Pilot for all the places in the known world.
London.   1

QUARTO.

14 Hawkesworth's Account of the Voyages undertaken
    by the Order of his present Majesty for mak-
    ing Discoveries in the Southern Hemisphere,
    and successively performed by commodore
    Byron, captain Wallis, captain Carteret, and
    captain Cooke.   Illustrated with cuts, maps,
    charts, &c.   London, 1773.   3

OCTAVO.

I. J.

FOLIO.

OCTAVO.

DUODECIMO.

K.

DUODECIMO.

L.

OCTAVO.

M.

QUARTO.

OCTAVO.

No.   Vols.

11   Morse's American Gazetteer; exhibiting the States, Provinces, Towns, &c. &c. on the American Continent, also of the West-India Islands, and other islands appendant to the continent, and those newly discovered in the Pacific Ocean. London, 1798.   1

60   Mackenzie's Voyages from Montreal on the river St. Laurence through the Continent of North America, to the Frozen and Pacific Oceans; in the years 1789 and 1793, with a preliminary account of the rise, progress and present state of the fur trade of that country. Illustrated with maps. London, 1802.   2

62   Meares' Voyages made in the years 1788 and 1789, from China to the North West Coast of America, with observations on the probable existence of a North West passage, and some account of the trade between the North West Coast of America and China; and the latter country and Great Britain. London, 1791.   2

74   Muirhead's Travels in Parts of the late Austrian Low Countries, France, the Pays de Vaud, and Tuscany, in 1787 and 1789. London, 1803.   1

93   Macnevin's Ramble through Swisserland in the Summer and Autumn of 1802. Dublin, 1803.   1

100   M'Callum's Travels in Trinidad, during the months of February, March, and April, 1803. Liverpool, 1805.   1

P.

QUARTO

34   Portlock's Voyage round the World; but more particularly to the North-West coast of America, performed in 1785, 6, 7 and 1788. Embellished with plates. London, 1789.   1

46   Pinkerton's Collection of Voyages and Travels, forming a complete history of the origin and progress of discovery, by sea and land, from the earliest ages to the present time. Illustrated by numerous engravings. Philadelphia, 1809.

1   Pinkerton's Modern Geography, or a Description of the Empires, Kingdoms, States and Colonies; with the oceans, seas and isles, in all parts of the world, including the most recent discoveries and political alterations. Philadelphia, 1804.   2

S.

QUARTO.

OCTAVO.

T.

QUARTO.

U.

OCTAVO.

V.

QUARTO.

OCTAVO.

W.

OCTAVO.

LAW.

A.

FOLIO.

OCTAVO.

DUODECIMO.

B.

FOLIO.

E.
OCTAVO.

73 Espinasse's Reports of Cases argued and ruled at Nisi Prius, in the Courts of King's Bench and Common Pleas, from Easter Term, 1793, to Hilary Term, 1799. Day's edition, 4 vols. in 2. Hartford, 1808.   2

184 East's Treatise on the Pleas of the Crown. London, 1806.   2

DUODECIMO.

6 Elsynge on the Manner of holding Parliaments in England. London, 1768.   1

F.
OCTAVO.

180 Foster's Discourses upon a few Branches of the Crown Law, and a Report of Proceedings on the Commission for the Trial of the Rebels in the year 1746, and other Crown Cases, &c. London, 1792.   1

244 Fraser's Reports of the Proceedings before Select Committees of the House of Commons, upon controverted elections. London. 1791.   1

250 Frederician Code; or a Body of Law for the dominions of the King of Prussia, founded on reason, and the constitutions of the country. Translated from the French. Edinburgh, 1761. 2

285 La Scienza della Legislazione, del Cavalier Gaetano Filangieri. Siciliana.   9

G.
FOLIO.

2 Grotius on the Rights of War and Peace, in three books. Wherein are explained, the Law of Nature and Nations, and the principal points relating to government. Translated from the Latin, with the notes of M. Barbeyrac. London, 1738.   1

DUODECIMO.

14 Glanvilla's Tractatus de Legibus et Consuetudinibus Regni Angliæ, tempore Regis Henrici Secundi. London, 1673.   1

H.
QUARTO.

27 Hatsell's Precedents of Proceedings in the House of Commons, &c. with observations. Second edition, 2 sets, 2 vols. each. London, 1785.   4

M.

OCTAVO.

DUODECIMO.

No.   Vols.

15 Mably sur le Droit Public de l'Europe, &c. A
     Geneve, 1776.   3

N.

DUODECIMO.

26 Nouveau Commentaire sur l'Ordonnance de la
     Marine, du Mois d'Août, 1685. A Marseille,
     1780.   2

O.

OCTAVO.

222 Oldfield's History of the Original Constitution of
      Parliaments, from the time of the Britons to
      the present day. London, 1797.   1

DUODECIMO.

30 Orders and Resolutions of the House of Com-
     mons, on controverted elections and returns.
     London, 1734.   1

P.

FOLIO.

1 Puffendorff's Law of Nature and Nations: or a
    General System of the most important princi-
    ples of Morality, Jurisprudence and Politics.
    Translated from the Latin, by Basil Kennet,
    with notes, &c. by M. Barbeyrac. London,
    1749.   1

18 Petyt's Jus Parliamentarium: or the Ancient Pow-
     er, Jurisdiction, Rights and Liberties of the
     most high Court of Parliament. London,
     1739.   1

OCTAVO.

83 Peters's Admiralty Decisions in the District Court
     of the United States, for the Pennsylvania
     District. Philadelphia, 1807.   2

90 Principles of Penal Law. London, 1771.   1

238 Powell's Essay upon the Law of Contracts and
      Agreements. Walpole, (N. H.) 1809.   1

255 Pothier's Treatise on Obligations, considered in a
      Moral and Legal View. Translated from the
      French. Newbern, (N. C.) 1802.   1

256 Plowden's Jura Anglorum, or the Rights of En-
      glishmen. Dublin, 1792.   1

DUODECIMO.

7 Petyt's Discourse on the Ancient Right of the
    Commons of England, &c. London, 1680.   1

No.   Vols.

8   Petyt's Miscellanea Parliamentaria, &c.   London,
      1671.   1

R.

FOLIO.

12   Rolle's Abridgment des plusieurs Cases et Resolu-
       tions del Common Ley.   London, 1668.   1
17   Ryley's Placita Parliamentaria, &c.   Londini, 1661.   1
44   Reports of Cases argued and determined in the
       Court of King's Bench, in Michelmas Term in
       the twenty sixth year of George the Third,
       1785. By Charles Durnford and Edward Hyde
       East.   London, 1786.   1

OCTAVO.

80   Robinson's Reports of Cases argued and deter-
       mined in the High Court of Admiralty, from
       1798 to 1801.   London, 1802.   *See also No.*
       193.   3
102 Rutherford's Institutes of Natural Law, being the
       substance of a course of lectures on Grotius de
       Jure Belli et Pacis.   Cambridge, 1754.   2
108 Reeve's History of the English Law, from the time
       of the Saxons to the end of the reign of Philip
       and Mary. 2 sets, 4 vols each. London, 1787.   8
214 Reeve's History of the Law of Shipping and Navi-
       gation.   London, 1792.   1
265 Report of the Committee appointed to inquire into
       the Official Conduct of Samuel Chase, and of
       Richard Peters, &c. &c. 2 copies, 1804.   2

S.

FOLIO.

13   Scobell's Collection of Acts and Ordinances of
       Parliament, from the year 1640 to the year
       1656.   London, 1658.   1
43   Spelman's Works relating to the Laws and Anti-
       quities of England.   London, 1727.   1

OCTAVO.

91   Swift's System of the Laws of the State of Con-
       necticut.   Windham, 1795.   2
194 Story's Selection of Pleadings in Civil Actions,
       subsequent to the declaration. with occasional
       annotations on the law of pleading.   Salem,
       1805.   1

No.   Vols.

252   Williams's Digest of the Statute Law, comprising
        the substance and effect of all the public acts of
        Parliament in force, from Magna Charta, in the
        ninth year of king Henry the Third, to the
        twenty-seventh year of the reign of George the
        Third, inclusive.   London, 1788.   1

279   Wilson's Lectures on Law, delivered in the College
        of Philadelphia, in the years 1790 and 1791.
        Philadelphia, 1804.   3

STATE LAWS.

Laws of New Hampshire.   Printed by Melcher, 1792.

Constitution and Laws of New Hampshire, published in pur-
    suance of a Resolution of December, 1804.

Revised Statutes of Vermont, 1791.

Laws of the State of Vermont, revised and passed in 1797.
    Printed by Josiah Fay, 1798.

Perpetual Laws of Massachusetts, from 1780 to 1789.

Ditto, from 1789 to 1792.

Ditto, from 1780 to 1800.   2 vols.

Private and Special Statutes of Massachusetts, from 1780 to
    1805.   3 vols.

Acts and Laws of Connecticut.   Printed in 1784.

Ditto.

Laws of Rhode Island, passed in 1774, 5, 6, 7 and 1778.   2
    vols.

Revised Laws of Rhode Island.   Printed 1798.

Ditto.

Laws passed January, 1798, to December, 1802, inclusive.

Ditto.

Laws of New York, from the first to the twelfth Session of
    the Legislature, inclusive.   Published according to the
    Act of 1786.   2 vols.

Same.

Revised Code of 1801.   2 vols.

Ditto.

Ditto continued, 3d and 4th vols.

Laws of New Jersey.   Acts of the General Assembly.   Com-
                        piled by S. Allington, 1776.
                        Ditto.   Compiled by P. Wilson, 1784.
                        Ditto, from October, 1791, to Octo-
                        ber, 1797, inclusive.   4 vols.
                        Acts of the General Assembly.   Re-
                        vised by W. Patterson, 1800.
                        Same.

Laws of Pennsylvania. Charters and Acts of Assembly. Published by Miller and Co. 1762.

Charters and Acts of Assembly. Hall & Sellers, printers, 1775.

Same.

Ditto, by Order of the General Assembly, by T. M'Kean. Baily, printer, 1782.

Collection of Laws, commencing October, 1783, to April, 1790. Bradford, printer.

Laws of the Commonwealth, republished by J. Dallas, 1797. 4 vols.

Same.

Ditto. By Carey and Bioren, 1803. 6 vols.

Laws of Maryland. Bacon's edition, 1765.

Ditto. Hanson's edition, 1787.

Same.

Laws passed in 1785, 6, 7, 8, 9, 1790 and 1791.

Herty's Digest to the End of November Session, 1797.

Kilty's edition, 1790, 2 vols.

Same.

Laws of Virginia. Acts of the General Assembly, October, 1779.

Acts of the General Assembly, 1784.

Ditto, 1788.

Ditto. Printed by Dunlap and Hayes, 1792.

Revised Code. Printed by A. Davis, 1794.

Ditto. Printed by Saml. Pleasants, junr. 1808. 2 vols.

Laws of North Carolina, revised by Order of the Assembly, 1751.

Ditto. Revised by I. Iredell, 1791.

Same.

Ditto. Revised by F. X. Martin, 1804.

Laws of South Carolina, of the Session in 1788.

Ditto. Grimke's edition, to 1790.

Ditto. Ratified, 1791.

Laws of Georgia. Marbury and Crawford's Digest.

Laws of the United States. 250 sets, containing 10 vols. each set.

300 sets of the Journals of the Old Congress, 13 vols. each set.

300 copies of Lambert's Precedents of Order, published in pursuance of a Resolution of the House of Representatives of the 26th of April, 1810.

Herty's Digest of the United States' Laws. 2 copies.

250 copies of the Laws relating to the Public Lands, deposited in the Library by virtue of an act passed February 18, 1811.]

ETHICS; OR THE MORAL SYSTEM IN GENERAL, THEOLOGY AND MYTHOLOGY.

A.

QUARTO.

No.   Vols.

5   Aristotle's Ethics and Politics, comprising his
      practical philosophy, &c. Translated from the
      Greek, by John Gillies. London, 1797.   2

OCTAVO.

39   An Exposition of Christian Doctrine, as taught in
      the Protestant Church of the United Brethren,
      or Unitas Fratrum. Written in German, by
      A. G. Spangenberg; with a preface by Benja-
      min La Trobe. London, 1796.   1

B.

OCTAVO.

4   Burgh on the Dignity of Human Nature, or an ac-
      count of the means of attaining the true end of
      our existence. London, 1794.   1

13   Beattie's Elements of Moral Science. Edinburgh,
      1807.   2

15   Beattie's Essay on the Nature and Immutability of
      Truth, in Opposition to Sophistry and Scepti-
      cism. London, 1807.   1

29   Bates's Christian Politics. London, 1806.   1

55   Bryant's Analysis of Antient Mythology, wherein
      an attempt is made to divest tradition of fable,
      and to reduce the truth to its original purity.
      London, 1807.   6

54   Branagan's Essay on the Oppression of the Exiled
      Sons of Africa, &c.   1

C.

OCTAVO.

52   Clarkson's History of the Rise, Progress, and Ac-
      complishment of the Abolition of the African
      Slave Trade, by the British Parliament. Phi-
      ladelphia, 1808. *The gift of the Philadelphia
      Society, for promoting the Abolition of Slavery.*   2

No.   Vols.

43 Clarkson's Portraiture of Quakerism, taken from
a view of the education and discipline, manners, religious principles, &c. of the Society of
Friends. New York, 1806.   6

16 Cato and Laelius, or Essays on Old Age and Friendship, by M. T. Cicero, with remarks by Wil-
liam Melmoth. London, 1795.   2

D.
OCTAVO.

30 Dunbar's Essays on the History of Mankind, in
Rude and Cultivated Ages. London, 1781.   1

E.
OCTAVO.

18 Ensor's Independent Man: or an Essay on the
Formation and Developement of those principles and faculties of the human mind which
constitute moral and intellectual excellence.
London, 1806.   2

50 Essay on National Pride. Translated from the
German of J. G. Zimmerman, by Samuel H.
Wilcocke. New-York, 1799.   1

F.
OCTAVO.

23 Ferguson's Essay on the History of Civil Society.
Basil, 1789.   1

48 Faber's Dissertation on the Prophecies relative to
the great period of 1260 years, &c. London,
1808.   2

H.
OCTAVO.

20 Hartley's Observations on Man, his Frame, his
Duty, and his Expectations. London, 1801.   3

24 Helvetius on Man, his Intellectual Faculties, and
his Education. Translated from the French,
by W. Hooper. Albion Press, 1810.   2

26 Helvetius on the Mind and its several Faculties.
Translated from the French. Albion Press,
1810.   1

61 A Mythological, Etymological and Historical Dictionary; extracted from the analysis of ancient
mythology, by William Howell. London,
1793.   1

I and J.
OCTAVO.

40 Jones's Illustrations of the Four Gospels, founded
on circumstances peculiar to our Lord and the
Evangelists.   London, 1808.   1

K.
OCTAVO.

51 Knox's Essays on some of the most Important
Christian Doctrines and Virtues.   Harrisburg,
1808.   1

M.
OCTAVO.

12 Millar's Observations concerning the Distinction
of Ranks in Society.   Edinburg, 1806.   1
28 Melancholy; as it proceeds from the dispositions
and habit, the passion of love, and the influence
of religion.   Drawn chiefly from the celebrated
work entitled Burton's Anatomy of Melancho-
ly.   London, 1801.   1

P.
OCTAVO.

7 Paley's Principles of Moral Philosophy.   London,
1799.   2 sets, 2 vols. each.   4
41 Paley's View of the Evidences of Christianity.
London, 1807.   2

R.
QUARTO.

2 Reid's Essays on the Intellectual Powers of Man.
Edinburgh, 1785.   1

S.
QUARTO.

1 Stuart's View of Society in Europe, in its progress
from rudeness to refinement; or Inquiries concerning the History of Law, Government, and
Manners.   London, 1783. Same work octavo,
No. 11.   2

OCTAVO.

1 Shaftesbury's Characteristicks of Men, Manners,
Opinions, Times.   By John Baskerville.
Birmingham, 1793.   3

No.   Vols.

5 Smith's Theory of Moral Sentiments, with a dissertation on the origin of languages. London,
   1797.   2
27 Stael (the Baroness) on the Influence of the Pas-
   sions upon the Happiness of Individuals and of
   Nations. Translated from the French. London, 1798.   1

OCTAVO.

31 The Koran; commonly called the Alcoran of
   Mahommed. Translated from the original
   Arabic. With notes and a preliminary discourse, by George Sale. London, 1801.   2
46 Towers's Illustrations of Prophecy, &c. &c. Philadelphia, 1808.   2

LOGIC, RHETORIC AND CRITICISM.

A.

OCTAVO.

50 Adams's (John Quincy) Lectures on Rhetoric and
   Oratory. Cambridge, 1810.   2
53 A Collection of Speeches, delivered in the British
   House of Commons by Mr. Burke, Mr. Fox,
   &c. &c. Presented by the Honorable L. Saw-
   yer.   1

B.

OCTAVO.

26 Blair's Lectures on Rhectoric and Belles Lettres.
   London, 1798.   3
45 Browne's British Cicero, or a Selection of the most
   admired Speeches in the English Language;
   to which is prefixed an introduction to the
   study and practice of eloquence. Philadelphia,
   1810.   3
56 Burke's Inquiry into the Origin of our Ideas, of
   the Sublime and Beautiful. With an introductory discourse concerning taste. Philadelphia,
   1806.   1

C.

OCTAVO.

29   Ciceronis Orationes quædam Selectæ, cum Inter-
pretatione et notis quas in usum Serenissimi
Delphini, &c. &c. Huic editioni accesserunt
dialogi de Senectute et de Amicitia. Editio
primo Americana, cura Milcolumbi Campbell.
Novi Eboraci, 1804.   1

30   Cicero's Orations, translated into English; with
notes historical and critical. By William Guthrie. London, 1806.   2

32   Cicero on Oratory and Orators, with explanatory
notes. London, 1808.   2

39   Curran's Speeches; or, Sketches of Trials in Ireland for High Treason, &c. Baltimore, 1805,
2 copies.   2

D.

OCTAVO.

55   Deinology; or, the Union of Reason and Ele-
gance; being instructions to a young barrister.
By Hortensius. London, 1789.   1

E.

OCTAVO.

1   Edinburgh Review, or Critical Journal, from October 1802, to January 1809, inclusive.   13

48   Eloquence of the British Senate; being a selection
of the best speeches of the most distinguished
English, Irish, and Scotch Parliamentary Spea-
kers, from the beginning of the reign of
Charles the First, to the present time; with
notes, &c. By John Hazlitt. New York, 1810. 2

52   Eulogies and Orations, on the Life and Death of
General George Washington. Boston, 1800.   1

F.

OCTAVO.

54   Ferdinando Fairfax's Oration, delivered in Charlestown in Virginia, on the fourth of July 1805.
Presented by the author.   1

L.
OCTAVO.

34 Leland's Translation of the Orations of Demosthenes, pronounced to excite the Athenians against Philip King of Macedon. London, 1770.   3

37 Longinus on the Sublime. Translated from the Greek, with notes and observations, by William Smith. London, 1800.   1

38 Dionysii Longini de Sublimate, &c. Zacharias Pearce. Amstelædami, 1733.   1

M.
OCTAVO.

14 Monthly Review: or, Literary Journal, from July 1775, to September, 1781, inclusive.   10

P.
OCTAVO.

41 Pitt's Speeches in the House of Commons, &c. London, 1806.   4

Q.
OCTAVO.

24 Quinctillian's Institutes of Eloquence; or, the Art of Speaking in Public, in every Character and Capacity. Translated from the Latin, by W. Guthrie. London, 1805.   2

W.
OCTAVO.

57 Wirt's Two Principal Arguments on the Trial of Aaron Burr, for High Treason. Richmond, 1808.   1

DICTIONARIES, GRAMMARS AND TREATISES ON EDUCATION.

A.

OCTAVO.

7 Ash's Complete Dictionary of the English Language, &c. London, 1775.   1

8 Same Work. London, 1795.   2

OCTAVO.

No.   Vols.

16 Dufief's Universal and Pronouncing Dictionary of the French and English Languages. Philadelphia, 1810.   3

21 Dibdin's Introduction to the Knowledge of Rare and Valuable Editions of the Greek and Latin Classics, Lexicons, Grammars, &c. &c. London, 1804.   1

29 Delaware Indian and English Spelling-book. By David Zeisberger. Philadelphia, 1806. Presented in behalf of the Society of the United Brethren, by John G. Cunow, Esq.   1

E.

OCTAVO.

1 Eber's Complete Dictionary of the German and English Languages. Leipzig, 1796. 5

18 Epea Pteroenta; or, the Diversions of Purley. By John Horne Tooke. Philadelphia, 1806. 2

G.

QUARTO.

8 Græcum Lexicon Manuale, a Benjamine Hedrico, &c. Londini, 1803.   1

H.

OCTAVO.

25 Hermes, or a Philosophical Inquiry concerning Universal Grammar. By James Harris. London, 1806.   1

J.

QUARTO.

10 Johnson's Dictionary of the English Language, to which are prefixed a history of the language, and an English grammar. London, 1799. 2
With an octavo supplement, No. 6. By George Mason. New York, 1803.   1

L.

FOLIO.

1 Lyle's Dictionarium Saxonico et Gothico-Latinum. Londini, 1772.   2

OCTAVO.

No.   Vols.

22 Lempriere's Classical Dictionary, containing a full
      account of all the proper names mentioned in
      ancient authors.   Dublin, 1792.   1

28 Lancaster's System of Education, &c. &c.   New
      York, 1807.   1

27 Neef's ditto ditto.   Philadelphia, 1808.   1

P.

OCTAVO.

12 Parkhurst's Greek and English Lexicon, to the
      New Testament.   London, 1804.   1

S.

FOLIO.

6 Spelmanno's Glossarium, &c.   Londoni, 1687.   1

7 Skinner's Etymologicon Linguæ Anglicanæ, &c.
      Londini, 1671.   1

W.

OCTAVO.

10 Walker's Critical Pronouncing Dictionary of the
      English Language, &c. &c. Philadelphia, 1805,   1

20 Walker's Key to the Classical Pronunciation of
      Greek, Latin and Scripture proper names.   Lon-
      don, 1804.   1

23 Webster's Dissertations on the English Language.
      Boston, 1789.   1

GENERAL AND LOCAL POLITICS, POLITICAL ECONOMY, &c.

A.

OCTAVO.

27 Adams's Defence of the Constitutions of Govern-
      ment of the United States of America, against
      the attack of M. Thurgot in his Letter to Dr.
      Price.   London, 1794.   3

No.   Vols.

30   Same Work. Philadelphia, 1797.   2

47   An Account of the Proceedings of the British, and other Inhabitants, of the Province of Quebec, in order to obtain an House of Assembly in that Province. London, 1775.   2

59   An Examination of the British Doctrine, which subjects to Capture a Neutral Trade not open in time of Peace. Ascribed to James Madison, Esquire.   1

90   An Examination of the Conduct of Great Britain respecting Neutrals. Philadelphia, 1807.   1

94   A Political Account of the Island of Trinidad, from its Conquest by Sir Ralph Abercrombie, in 1797, to the present time; in a letter to the Duke of Portland. By a gentleman of the island. London, 1807.   1

B.
OCTAVO.

13   Brougham's Inquiry into the Colonial Policy of the European Powers. Edinburgh, 1803.   2

24   Burgh's Political Disquisitions; or an Inquiry into Public Errors, Defects and Abuses. London, 1774.   3

35   Bristed's Hints on the National Bankruptcy of Britain, and on her resources to maintain the present contest with France. New York, 1809.   1

43   Bolingbroke's Letters and Correspondence, during the time he was Secretary of State to Queen Anne. London, 1798.   4

82   Blodget's Statistical Manual for the United States. Washington City, 1806.   1

C.
OCTAVO.

21   Colquhoun on the Police of London; containing a detail of the various crimes and misdemeanors by which public and private property and security are, at present, injured and endangered; and suggesting remedies for their prevention. London, 1805.   1.

34   Comber's Inquiry into the State of National Subsistence, as connected with the Progress of Wealth and Population. London, 1808.   1

91   Census of the United States for 1791 and 1800. Washington City, 1802.   1

81 Gallatin's Sketch of the Finances of the United
     States. New York, 1796.   1

I. & J.

OCTAVO.

15 Jarrold's Dissertations on Man, in Answer to Mal-
     thus on Population. London, 1806.   1

L.

OCTAVO.

20 Lauderdale's Inquiry into the Nature and Origin
     of Public Wealth, and into the means and causes
     of its increase. Edinburgh, 1804.   1

DUODECIMO.

99 Lettres et Négociations entre M. Jean de Witt
     et Messieurs les Plenipotentiares des Provinces
     Unis des Pais Bas, &c. &c. A Amsterdam,
     1725.   5
104 Lettres et Négociations de Monsieur le Comte
     d'Estrades. A Bruxelles, 1709.   5
110 Les Négociations de Monsieur le Président Jean-
     nin. A Paris, 1659.   2

M.

OCTAVO.

9 Malthus on the Principle of Population, or a View
    of its past and present Effects on Human Hap-
    piness, &c. &c. 2 sets, 2 vols. each. London,
    1806.   4
60 Monroe's View of the Conduct of the Executive,
     in the Foreign Affairs of the United States,
     connected with the Mission to the French Re-
     public, during the years 1794, 5 and 6. Phila-
     delphia, 1797.   1
61 Message of the President of the United States of
     America to Congress, relative to the French
     Republic; delivered January 19, 1797.   1
62 Ditto, on the Subject of the Attack on the Chesa-
     peake, &c. &c.   1
63 Ditto, relative to France and Great Britain; deli-
     vered December 5, 1793.   1
64 Ditto, to both Houses of Congress, at the opening
     of the Second Session of the Tenth Congress,
     on the 8th November, 1808. 2 copies.   2

N.

OCTAVO.

P.

OCTAVO.

R.

FOLIO.

OCTAVO.

83 Récueil des Déductions, Manifestes, Déclarations, Traités, &c. &c. qui ont été rédigés et publiés pour la Cour de Prusse, par le Ministre d'Etat Comte de Hertzberg, depuis le commencement de la guerre de sept ans, 1756, jusqu'à celui de la guerre de Baviere, 1778. A Paris.   3

S.

QUARTO.

1 Sydney's (Algernon) Discourses on Government, &c. London, 1772.   1

    Same work, octavo, No. 1, with an account of the Author's Life New York, 1805.   3

2 Steuart's Inquiry into the Principles of Political Economy, being an Essay on the Science of Domestic Policy in Free Nations, &c. London, 1767.   2

4 Sinclair's History of the Public Revenue of the British Empire London, 1785.   1

    Same work, octavo, No. 19. Dublin, 1785.   1

OCTAVO.

4 Smith's Inquiry into the Nature and Causes of the Wealth of Nations. London, 1799.   3

7 Same work, with notes, &c. by William Playfair. Hartford (Conn), 1811.   2

36 State Papers for 1808, 9; containing a Letter from the Secretary of State to Mr. Monroe, on the subject of the attack on the Chesapeake; the Correspondence of Mr. Monroe with the British Government; and also Mr. Madison's Correspondence with Mr. Rose on the same subject.   1

38 Somers (Lord) on the Rights, Power, and Prerogative of Kings, and the Rights, Privileges and Properties of the People, &c. &c. London, 1771.   1

40 Somerville's History of Political Transactions, and of Parties, from the Restoration of Charles the Second, to the death of King William. Dublin, 1793.   1

80 Steele's Tables of the British Custom and Excise Duties, &c. London, 1799.   1

No.   Vols.
77 Woodward's Considerations on the Executive Go-
    vernment of the United States of America.   2
    copies.   Flatbush, (N. Y.) 1809.   Presented
    by the author.   2

TRADE AND COMMERCE.

A.

QUARTO.

1   Anderson's Historical and Chronological Deduc-
    tion of the Origin of Commerce, from the ear-
    liest accounts to the present time.   London,
    1787.   4

20 Same work, 8vo. continued to the year 1789.   By
    Mr. Coombe.   Dublin, 1790.   6

OCTAVO.

33 American Negotiator, or the Various Currencies of
    the British Colonies in America, reduced into
    English money.   By J. Wright, London, 1761.   1

34 An Essay on the Commerce of Portugal and her
    Colonies, particularly of Brasil in South
    America.   Translated from the Portuguese of
    J. J. Da Cunha de Azeredo Coutinho.   Lon-
    don, 1801.   1

B.

OCTAVO.

29 Beaujour's View of the Commerce of Greece,
    formed after an annual average, from 1787 to
    1797.   Translated from the French, by Thomas
    H. Horne.   London, 1800.   1

31 Barton on the Freedom of Navigation and Mari-
    time Commerce, &c. adapted more particularly
    to the United States.   Philadelphia, 1802.
    2 copies.   2

C.

OCTAVO.

30 Colquhoun on the Commerce of the river Thames,
    containing an historical view of the trade of
    the port of London, &c.   London, 1800.   4

40   Child on Trade.   London, 1694. 12mo.   1

D.
OCTAVO.

7   Dictionary of Merchandise and Nomenclature in
    all Languages, containing the history, places
    of growth, culture and use, of such natural pro-
    ductions, as form articles of commerce; with
    their names in all European languages.   Phi-
    ladelphia, 1805.   1

9   D'Avenant's Political and Commercial Works,
    relating to the trade and revenue of England.
    Revised by Charles Whitworth.   London,
    1771.   5

G.
DUODECIMO.

39   Gee on the Trade and Navigation of Great Bri-
     tain.   London, 1767.   Presented by Doctor
     S. L. Mitchill.   1

H.
OCTAVO.

8   Hamilton's Introduction to Merchandise.   Edin-
    burgh, 1799.   1

37   Histoire Raisonnée du Commerce de la Russie.
     Par M. Sherer.   A Paris, 1788.   2

I. and J.
OCTAVO.

35   Jackson's Reflections on the Commerce of the
     Mediterranean, deduced from actual expe-
     rience, &c.   New-York, 1806.   1

L.
FOLIO.

3   Lex Mercatoria Rediviva, or the Merchant's Di-
    rectory.   By W. Beawes.   Fifth edition.   Lon-
    don, 1792.   1

1   Same work, 8vo.   Dublin, 1795.   2

OCTAVO.

3   Lex Mercatoria Americana, or an Inquiry into the
    Law Merchant of the United States.   New-
    York, 1802.   3

No.   Vols.

36 L'Indépendence Absolue des Americaines des
     Etats-Unis. Prouvée par l'état actuel de leur
     commerce avec les nations Européennes. A
     Paris, 1798.   1

M.

FOLIO.

4 Malyne's Ancient Law Merchant. London, 1686.   1
5 Mortimer's Dictionary of Trade and Commerce.
    London, 1766.   1

QUARTO.

5 Macpherson's Annals of Commerce, containing the
    commercial transactions of the British empire
    and other countries, from the earliest accounts
    to the meeting of the Union Parliament in
    January, 1801. London, 1805.   4

OCTAVO.

4 Montefiore's Commercial Dictionary, containing
    the present state of mercantile law, practice
    and custom. With additions relative to the
    laws, usages and practice of the United
    States. Philadelphia, 1804.   3
18 Mortimer's Lectures on the Elements of Com-
     merce, &c. London, 1801. 2 copies.   2

O.

OCTAVO.

14 Oddy's European Commerce, showing new and
     secure channels of trade with the continent of
     Europe, detailing the produce, manufactures,
     and commerce of Russia, Prussia, Sweden,
     Denmark and Germany, &c. &c. Philadel-
     phia, 1807. 2 sets, 2 vols. each.   4

P.

FOLIO.

1 Postlethwayt's Universal Dictionary of Trade and
    Commerce. Fourth edition. London, 1774.   2

S.

26 Sheffield (Lord) on the Commerce of the Ameri-
     can States. London, 1784—3 copies.   3

MILITARY AND NAVAL TACTICS.

QUARTO.

AGRICULTURE, RURAL ECONOMY, &c.

OCTAVO.

NATURAL HISTORY, NATURAL AND EXPERIMEN- TAL PHILOSOPHY, &c.

FOLIO.

No.   Vols.

2 Wilson's American Ornithology, or the Natural
   History of the Birds of the United States.
   Illustrated with plates engraved and colored
   from original drawings taken from nature.
   Philadelphia, 1808.

QUARTO.

1 Smellie's Philosophy of Natural History. Edinburgh, 1790.   1
2 Nicholson's Journal of Natural Philosophy, &c.
   Illustrated with engravings. London, 1797.   5

OCTAVO.

1 Saint Pierre's Studies of Nature. Translated by
   Henry Hunter. With original notes and illustrations by Benjamin Smith Barton. Philadelphia, 1808.   3
4 Kirwan's Geological Essays. London, 1799.   1
5 Buffon's Natural History. Barr's edition. London, 1797.   16
21 Anderson's General History of Quadrupeds. With
   figures engraved on wood, &c. New-York,
   1804.   1
22 Wilkinson's Elements of Galvanism, in theory and
   practice, with a view of its history from the
   first experiments of Galvani to the present
   time. London, 1804.   2
24 Cavallo on Electricity, with original experiments,
   &c. London, 1795.   3
27 Hutton's Recreations in Natural Philosophy and
   Mathematics. London, 1803.   4
31 Hooper's Recreations in Numbers and Natural
   Philosophy. London, 1794.   4
36 Rumford's Philosophical Papers, or a Collection
   of Experimental Investigations relating to
   various branches of Natural Philosophy and
   Mechanics. London, 1802.   1
37 Smith's (Samuel Stanhope) Essay on the Causes
   of the Variety of Complexion and Figure in the
   Human Species. New Brunswick, 1810.   1
38 Smith's (Adam) Essays on Philosophical Subjects. Dublin, 1795.   1

MEDICINE, SURGERY AND CHEMISTRY.

OCTAVO

No.   Vols.

No.		Vols.
42	Chaptal's Chemistry applied to the Arts and Manufactures. London, 1807.	4
46	Black's Lectures on the Elements of Chemistry, delivered in the University of Edinburgh. Philadelphia, 1807.	3
49	Parkes' Chemical Catechism, or the Application of Chemistry to the Arts. Philadelphia, 1807.	1
50	Henry's Epitome of Chemistry, 12mo. Philadelphia, 1802.	1

POETRY AND THE DRAMA, WORKS OF FICTION, WIT, &c.

FOLIO.

1	The Fables of John Dryden, ornamented with engravings from the pencil of Lady Diana Beauclerc. London, 1797.	1

QUARTO.

2	Barlow's Columbiad. Philadelphia, 1807.	1
3	Poetry of the Anti-Jacobin. London, 1801.	1

OCTAVO.

4	Poetical Translations. London,	3
7	Same Work, 2 vols.	2
9	The Poetical Works of John Milton; with the principal notes of various commentators; and some account of the life of Milton, by the Rev. Henry John Todd. London, 1801.	6
15	Gifford's Translation of the Satires of Decimus Junius Juvenalis, with notes and illustrations. London, 1806.	1
16	Same Work, American edition. Philadelphia, 1803.	2
18	Sotheby's Translation of the Georgics of Virgil. London, 1800.	1
19	Moore's (Thomas) Poems, Odes, &c. Philadelphia, 1806.	1

No.   Vols.
145 The Judge, a Poem, by the Rev. Jerome Alley.
       London, 1803.   1
146 Rabelais' Works. Translated from the French,
       by Du Chat, Motteux and others. London,
       1807.   4
150 Don Quixotte, with the Life of Cervantes. By
       Dr. Smollett. Dublin.   5
155 Marmontel's Moral Tales. London, 1800.   3
158 Knickerbocker's History of New York, &c. 1809.   2
160 Brooke's Fool of Quality. Baltimore, 1810.   2
162 More's Utopia. London, 1795.   1
163 My Pocket Book. New York, 1807.   1

ARTS AND SCIENCES, AND MISCELLANEOUS LITERATURE.

A.

OCTAVO.

146 American Museum, for the years 1790, 1792 and
       1798. By Mathew Carey. Philadelphia.   5
242 Ames (Fisher) The Works of, compiled by a num-
       ber of his friends. With notices of his life and
       character. Boston, 1809. 2 copies.   2

B.

QUARTO.

50   Bacon's Works. London, 1778.   5
55   Burke's Works. London, 1792.   3
58   Bibliotheca Americana; or, a Chronological Cata-
       logue of the most curious and interesting Books,
       Pamphlets, State Papers, &c. upon the Subject
       of North and South America, from the Earliest
       Period to the Present, in Print and Manuscript,
       &c. &c. London, 1789.   1

OCTAVO.

136 Burke's Works. First American, from the last
       London edition. Boston, 1806.   4

No.		Vols.
156	Bynkershoek's Works. Lugduni Batavorum, 1752.	6
197	Bacon's Works. London, 1803.	10
319	Beckman's History of Inventions and Discoveries. Translated from the German. By William Johnston. London, 1797.	3

DUODECIMO.

| 121 | Recueil de Discours sur diverses Matières Import- antes. Par Jean Barbeyrac. A Amsterdam, 1731. | 2 |

C.

FOLIO.

| 36 | Chambers' Dictionary of Arts and Sciences. With a supplement and modern improve- ments. By Abraham Rees. Dublin, 1787. | 5 |

QUARTO.

| 76 | Delle Misure d'Ogni Genere Antiche e Moderne. Di G. F. Cristiani. In Venezia, 1760. | 1 |

OCTAVO.

| 266 | Cicero's (Marcus Tullius) Letters to Several of his Friends. With remarks by William Melmoth. London, 1804. | 3 |
| 322 | Coleman's Collection of the Facts and Documents, relative to the Death of General Alexander Hamilton. Together with the Orations, Ser- mons, &c. that have been written on his life and character. New York, 1804. | 1 |

D.

FOLIO.

| 1 | Diderot's Encyclopedie, ou Dictionnaire Raisonné des Sciences et des Arts. A Paris, 1751. | 35 |

QUARTO.

| 1 | Dobson's Encyclopædia. 2 sets, 18 volumes each. | 36 |
| 59 | Dictionnaire Universel des Sciences Morale, Eco- nomique, Politique et Diplomatique. A Lon- dres, 1777. | 30 |

F.
OCTAVO.

DUODECIMO.

G.
OCTAVO.

H.
OCTAVO.

DUODECIMO.

115 Harris' Minor Encyclopedia, or Cabinet of Gene-
     ral Knowledge. Boston, 1803.   4

I. J.

QUARTO.

42 The Works of Sir William Jones. London, 1799. 8

OCTAVO.

174 The Works of Sir William Jones. With the life
     of the author. By Lord Teignmouth. London,
     1807.   13

DUODECIMO.

58 The Works of Samuel Johnson; with an essay on
    his life and genius by Arthur Murphy. Lon-
    don, 1806.   12

119 The Letters of Junius complete: interspersed with
     the letters and articles to which he replied.
     Also a prefatory inquiry respecting the real
     author, by John Almon. London, 1806.   2

L.

OCTAVO.

151 Leyden Gazette for January, 1807. 2 copies.   2
153 Lavater's Essays on Physiognomy, &c. Translat-
     ed from the German, by Thomas Holcroft.
     London, 1789.   3
188 The Works of John Locke. London, 1794.   9

DUODECIMO.

124 Lecteur François; ou, Recueil de Pieces pour ser-
     vir à perfectionner les Jeunes Gens dans la
     Lecture, &c. &c. Par Lindley Murray. A
     New York, 1803.   1

M.

QUARTO.

37 Memoirs of the American Academy of Arts and
    Sciences. Boston, 1793.   2
39 The Works of Andrew Marvell, Poetical, Contro-
    versial, and Political. With the life of the
    author by Edward Thompson. London, 1776.   3

OCTAVO.

220 The Works of Nicholas Machiavel. Translated
     from the originals, with notes, &c. By E.
     Farneworth. London, 1775.   4

No.   Vols.

Mitchill and Miller's Repository and Review of Philosophical Subjects, in the United States, and other parts of America. *See page* 83.   18

244 Miller's Retrospect of the Eighteenth Century; containing a sketch of the revolutions and improvements in science, arts, and literature, during that period. New York, 1803   2

324 Mansfield's Mathematical and Physical Essays, &c. New Haven.   1

325 Memorial of the Chesapeake and Delaware Canal Company.   1

DUODECIMO.

37 Œuvres complètes de Mably. A Paris, 1790.   21

126 Manuel Pratique et Elementaire des Poids et Mesures, &c. Par S. A. Tarbé. A Paris, 1803.   1

N.

OCTAVO.

65 New England Quarterly Magazine for 1802. Boston.   1

P.

OCTAVO.

269 Pliny's Letters, with occasional remarks. By William Melmoth. London, 1805.   2

276 Porcupine's Works, exhibiting a faithful picture of the United States of America, &c. &c. &c. By William Cobbett. London, 1801.   12

DUODECIMO.

121 Patriotic Addresses to John Adams, President of the United States, together with his Answers, in 1798. Boston.   1

R.

OCTAVO.

246 Rumford's Essays, Political, Economical, and Philosophical. London, 1800.   2

295 The Repertory of Arts and Manufactures, &c. Selected from the Transactions of the Philosophical Societies of all Nations. London.   23

DUODECIMO.

125 Rochefaucault's Maxims and Moral Reflections. London, 1802.   1

S.

FOLIO.

OCTAVO.

DUODECIMO

T.

OCTAVO.

V.

OCTAVO.

DUODECIMO.

W.

OCTAVO.

271 Wanley's Wonders of the Little World, or, a General History of Man, &c.   London, 1806.   **2**

GAZETTES.

Gazette of the United States, by Fenno, from April 15, 1789,
to May 30, 1793, 3 vols.

From June 1794, to June 1795, 2 vols.

For the year 1796, 2 vols.

Ditto for the years 1798 and 1799, 3 vols.

General Advertiser, by B. F. Bache, succeeded by W. Duane,
from October 1st, 1790, to December 31, 1794, 9 vols.

For the years 1796, 1799, 1800, 1801, and 1802, 5 vols.

Dunlap's American Daily Advertiser, for the years 1791,
1792, and 1793, 5 vols.

Claypole's Daily Advertiser, from November 1, 1791, to
June 1793, 2 vols.

From January 10, to July 7, 1794.

From January 1, 1798, to June, 1799, 2 vols.

Brown's Philadelphia Gazette, from January 1791, to June
1792, 2 vols.

From October 1792, to June, 1793.

From July, 1794, to December, 1796, 3 vols.

Porcupine's Gazette, from March, 1797, to June, 1799, 3 vols.

National Intelligencer, by Saml. H. Smith, succeeded by Joseph Gales, Jr. from October 31, 1800, to October 31,
1803, inclusive, 4 vols.

From November 1, 1806, to November 1, 1810, inclusive,
4 vols.

Washington Federalist, by Wm. A. Rind, from November,
1800, to February, 1801.

The Raleigh Star, by Thos. Henderson, for the year 1809.

MAPS, CHARTS AND PLANS.

MAPS.

Map of England and Wales. By Carey.	**1794**
Scotland.	**1789**

Map of Ireland, Civil and Ecclesiastical. By Beaufort. 1797
    France, divided into Departments.
    The New Discoveries in the Interior of North
        America. By A. Arrowsmith.   1795
    The Western part of North America. By
        Captain M. Lewis.   1805
    The United States. By Arrowsmith.   1796
    Ditto.   By A. Bradley.   1796
    Ditto.   Ditto.   1796
    Ditto.   Ditto.   1804
    Ditto.   Ditto.   1804
    The District of Maine. By Carleton.   1802
    Massachusetts, proper.   Ditto.   1802
    Ditto.   1802
    New York. By De Witt.   1802
    Ditto.   By Wm. M'Calpin.   1808
    Pennsylvania.   1775
    Ditto. By Reading Howell.   1792
    Maryland. By Griffith.   1794
    Virginia. By Fry and Jefferson.   1775
    Ditto.   By Bishop Madison.   1807
    North and South Carolina. By Mouzon.   1775
    North Carolina. By Price and Strother.   1807
    Southern Mail Route, from Washington, to New
        Orleans.   1807
    Orleans Territory. By Lafon.   1806
    South America. By Faden.   1799
    Upper Canada. By Smyth.   1800

CHARTS.

Chart of The World, Mercator's projection.   1790
    The Bay of Fundy, Nova Scotia, Cape Bre-
      ton, St. John's and Sable Island.
    The Coast of Nova Scotia, with the South coast
      of New Brunswick, including part of the is-
      land of St. John's and Cape Breton, and of
      the coast of New England. By Holland.   1787
    Gulph and River St. Lawrence, Nova Scotia,
      and the adjacent islands.   1787
    Newfoundland, and its Fishing Banks.   1789
    Coast of New England, from New York to
      Goldsborough Bay.   1787
    Nantucket Sound. By Captain Pinkham.   1791
    Long Island Sound. By Cahoone and Fosdick. 1805

Chart of Nantucket Harbor. By Coffin. 1794

    Coast of United States from New York to North Carolina. 1787

    Inland Navigation, from Cape Henry to Cape Roman. By Price and Strother. 1798

    North and South Carolina, Georgia and East Florida. 1787

    Bahama Banks, with the adjacent islands. 1787

    The Coast of North Carolina, between Cape Hatteras and Cape Fear. 1806

    Survey of the River St. Mary's from the Atlantic Ocean, being the boundary between the state of Georgia and East Florida. 1812

    Priestley's Chart of Biography.

    Ditto Chart of History.

PLANS.

Plan of Governor's Bedlow's and Oyster Islands, fortified for the defence of the harbor of New York.

Profile of the Works on Governor's Island.

Ditto of the Battery, &c. on Bedlow's Island.

Plan of the proposed works on Bedlow's Island.

Plan of Oyster Island and Fortifications.

Section of the Fort of Staten Island.

Plan of the City of Philadelphia, and its environs. Surveyed by John Hills, 1807

Plan of the City of Washington.

Plan, section, and elevation of the jail in the City of Washington.

RULES AND REGULATIONS

IN THE LIBRARY OF CONGRESS.

———

I. THE library shall be opened every day during the session of Congress, and for one week preceding and subsequent thereto, Sundays excepted, from nine o'clock in the morning to three o'clock in the afternoon, and from five o'clock to seven in the evening

II. In the recess of Congress, it shall be opened three days in every week, during the hours aforesaid, to wit: on Tuesday, Thursday and Saturday

III It shall be the duty of the Librarian to label and number the books, place them on the shelves, and preserve due lists and catalogues of the same He shall also keep due account and register of all issues and returns of books as the same shall be made, together with regular accounts of all expenses incident to the said library, and which are authorised by law.

IV. Books, to be issued by the Librarian pursuant to law, shall be returned as follows:

A folio within three ⎫ weeks;
A quarto within two ⎭
An octavo or duodecimo within one week:

And no member shall receive more than one folio, one quarto, or two octavos or duodecimos, within the terms aforesaid, unless where so connected as to be otherwise useless.

V. For all books issued to any person, except a mem·ber of Congress, a receipt or note shall be given, payable to the Librarian and his successors in office, of double the value thereof, as near as can be estimated, con-

13

ditioned to return the same, undefaced, within the term above mentioned, or to forfeit the amount of such note; at the expiration of which, unless application has been made by another person for the same book, and the Librarian requested to make a memorandum thereof, the said Librarian, upon the books being produced to him, may renew the issue for the same for the time and on the conditions aforesaid: *Provided,* That every receipt or note shall contain a further forfeiture or penalty for every day's detention of a book beyond the specified term, that is to say: for

A folio, one dollar per day;

A quarto fifty cents per day;

An octavo, twenty five cents per day:

And the same forfeiture or penalty shall be incurred by members of Congress for every illegal detention; which forfeiture or penalty may, for good cause be remitted by the President of the Senate and Speaker of the House of Representatives for the time being, in whole or in part. as the case may require.

VI. When a member shall prefer to take a book for the limited time, without removing it from the library, he shall be allowed to do so, and to preserve his priority for the use of such book for the time limited, in like manner as if he had withdrawn the book from the library: And the Librarian shall keep due account and entry of all such cases

VII. Books returned shall be delivered to the Librarian, to be examined whether damaged or not.

VIII If a book be returned damaged, the party returning it shall not be entitled to receive another until the damage for the first shall be satisfied

IX No book shall be issued within ten days of the termination of any session of Congress.

X. All books shall be returned five days before the close of a session, whether the time allowed for the use thereof be expired or not.

XI During the session of Congress, the Secretary of the Senate and Clerk of the House of Representatives, shall, on their respective responsibility, be entitled to receive for the use of their respective Houses, that is to say: the Secretary of the Senate six sets of the said laws and journals, and the Clerk of the House of Representatives eight sets; those for the Senate to be distributed, one set for the President's table, two sets for the Secretary's table, and the other three sets for committees of the Senate; those for the House of Representatives, one set for the Speaker's table, two sets for the Clerk's table, and one set for each of the standing committees of the House: which sets of laws and journals shall be duly returned to the Librarian by the said Secretary and Clerk, within three days after the close of the session for which they shall be drawn.

XII Whenever any person authorised thereto by law (except the President of the United States and members of Congress) shall receive from the library a set of the said laws and journals, he shall receipt therefor to the Librarian, conditioned to return the same undefaced to the library, five days before the close of that session of Congress for which they shall be drawn, under the penalty of double the value of each volume of laws or journals received, that is to say: for each volume of the laws and journals, valued at two dollars and a half per volume, in a penalty of five dollars per volume

XIII. One set of the said laws and journals shall be delivered by the Librarian to the President of the United States for his own use and the use of his successors in office, the President filing with the Librarian a written acknowledgment of the receipt of the same.

XIV. It shall be the duty of the Librarian to provide at public expense, a number of suitable boxes, equal to the number of individuals hereby authorised to receive from the library sets of the said laws and journals; each box to be provided with a lock and key, and delivered on application for the use of such persons as may draw in the manner aforesaid, in which to deposit and safely keep the books so by them respectively received, which boxes shall be returned to the library, together with the books, at the time and in the manner limited by the rules aforesaid.

XV   There shall be retained in the library all charts (the case of maps being specified in the act of January 26, 1802), plans of fortifications, buildings, or other designs in manuscript; volumes of plates or engravings; books accompanying the charts, plates or engravings; tables of chronology; volumes of newspapers; one set of the volumes of any encyclopedia or dictionary of the arts; one set of the volumes of any geographical work, gazetteers, dictionaries of language.   Of the above none shall be taken from the library, by any person, without special permission in writing from the President of the Senate and Speaker of the House of Representatives; except in cases where the presiding officer of either House may require any of them for the immediate use of the House.

XVI. The previous approbation of the President of the Senate, and Speaker of the House of Representatives shall be obtained for the purchase of articles for the use of the library, to be charged upon the contingent fund of the two Houses

XVII   It shall be the duty of the Librarian, four days before the termination of every session of Congress, to present to any member of Congress a list of the books which he has received from the library and not returned.

XVIII   The Librarian shall, three days before the termination of every session of Congress, furnish the Speaker of the House of Representatives and the Secretary of the Senate, with a list of the names of such members of Congress as shall not have returned the books received from the library, together with a description and value of such books, and also of the value of the set to which they may belong, and of the amount of fines with which they may stand charged; and it shall be the duty of the Speaker in settling the accounts of any such Representative, and of the Secretary of the Senate in settling the accounts of any such Senator, to retain a sum equal to double the value of the books retained, and if they shall form a part of a set, then double the value of the whole set; and also a sum equal to the fines with which such member may stand charged.

XIX Whenever any Senator or Representative shall obtain leave of absence for the remainder of any session of Congress, it shall be the duty of the Speaker of the House of Representatives, or of the Secretary of the Senate, as the case may be, to ascertain of the Librarian whether such Senator or Representative shall have returned the books which he may have received from the library, and have paid the fines which may have been incurred by him; and in case of failure, the same deduction shall be made in the settlement of the accounts of such Senator or Representative as are directed in the 18th rule

XX The Librarian shall collect all fines and forfeitures accruing upon notes given for books taken from the library.

XXI. All monies arising from fines and forfeitures shall constitute a part of the library fund, and shall be paid when required to the joint committee of the two Houses of Congress, who are charged with the disposition of that fund.

XXII. The Librarian shall, during the first week of every session, present to the joint committee of the two Houses of Congress, charged with the disposition of the library fund, an accurate statement of all monies received during the preceding year, arising from fines and forfeitures, under the foregoing rules.

Upon considering the subject of rules proper to be observed in the library of Congress, and examining and revising those heretofore adopted, we do order and direct that the foregoing be observed.

WM. H. CRAWFORD,
President of the Senate, pro tempore,

H. CLAY,
Speaker of the House of Representatives.

4th December, 1812.

Publication Note

The *Catalogue of the Books, Maps and Charts Belonging to the Library* . . . , here reproduced in facsimile, purported to describe the 3,076 volumes, as well as the maps, charts, and newspapers, held by the Library of Congress in 1812. At that time, there were no card catalogues, computer files, or reference staff. When a book was needed, for information, study, or entertainment, the printed book catalogue provided the only means of access to the contents of this library.

The holdings of the Library of Congress had been documented in earlier catalogues published in 1802 (with a supplement in 1803), 1804, and 1808. But these had included only brief titles which were grouped by size. The catalogue of 1812, as Robert Rutland explains in his essay, first introduced a classification scheme whereby the books, maps, and newspapers were arranged into sixteen subject and two format categories. Within broad classifications like "Ecclesiastical History," "Law," "Trade and Commerce," and "Gazettes," and with some attempt to maintain alphabetical order, the 1812 catalogue provided, in most cases, a shelf number, title, place and date of publication, and the number of volumes in the set.

The 1812 catalogue was probably prepared by the Joint Committee on the Library of Congress rather than by the Librarian of Congress. The Joint Committee controlled the Library's funds and was charged with the important task of selecting the books, while the Librarian's duties were essentially clerical. Printed by Roger C. Weightman, one of the several Washington printers who thrived on congressional contracts, the 1812 catalogue, supplemented by statutes and rules, was the last record of the Library of Congress before its destruction in 1814. The volume was probably bound in paper boards, measured 22 cm by 13 cm, and was printed in an edition of five hundred.

This publication is sponsored by the Center for the Book in the Library of Congress. The Center for the Book was established in 1977 to stimulate awareness of the importance of books, reading, and the printed word. Drawing on the resources of the Library of Congress, it brings together members of the book, educational, and business communities for symposia and projects. The center's major interests are the study of books in the past, present, and future; reading development and promotion; and the international role of books and the printed word. Its publications and programs are supported by tax-deductible contributions from individuals and corporations.

Reproduced from a copy of the original catalogue in the Rare Book and Special Collections Division, this publication was made possible by a fund established in honor of Verner W. Clapp, former Chief Assistant Librarian of Congress. To the facsimile we have added a historical introduction and three indexes. The volume was prepared under the direction of the staff of the Center for the Book: John Y. Cole, Executive Director, 1978– , and Judith O'Sullivan, Executive Director, 1981–1982. William Matheson, Chief, Rare Book and Special Collections Division, gave helpful advice. Leonard Beck, Rare Book and Special Collections Division, and Marvin Kranz, General Reading Rooms Division, assisted with the index. Special thanks go to Robert A. Rutland, who wrote the introduction.

The Library is grateful to Senator Howard H. Baker, Jr., and members of his staff, James M. Cannon, Lura Nell Triplett, and Emily Reynolds; and to the Architect of the

Capitol, George M. White, and members of his staff, Anne-Imelda Radice and Cynthia Pease Miller, for their efforts in the recreation of the first Library of Congress in the United States Capitol.

Lynda Corey Claassen
The Center for the Book

Index to Authors and Titles

Three indexes accompany this facsimile of the 1812 catalogue: a general index that includes the names of authors, editors, translators, reporters, titles, and Library of Congress main entries; an index to places of publication; and an index to dates of publication. Entries in the 1812 catalogue are brief and often erroneous. The indexes were designed to provide additional and correct information.

In preparing these three indexes, the indexer sought to find the full name of the author, the exact title, and the full imprint of the books listed in the catalogue. This effort was successful for all but four titles (each marked with an asterisk in the index). Since the books contained in the 1812 library were not themselves available for consultation, the indexer checked catalogue entries against such standard bibliographic tools as the Library of Congress card catalogue, the *National Union Catalog, Pre-1956 Imprints,* and the British Museum's *Catalogue of Printed Books.*

Index references include page numbers and, in parentheses, additional identifying information. In most cases, the additional information consists of the shelfmark printed to the left of catalogue entries. For example, 57(102) refers to item 102 on page 57. Occasionally, two items on the same page have identical shelfmarks; in these cases, the size of the volume (folio, quarto, octavo, duodecimo) has been added to the shelfmark, e.g., 64(1 octavo). When an item lacks a printed shelfmark, the first or other identifying word of the catalogue entry appears in parentheses, e.g., 19(Froissart's), 61(Public Lands), 93(*Raleigh Star*). These titles appear in the index as they were printed in the 1812 catalogue.

American Law Journal and Miscellaneous Repertory, 53(195)
The American Military Library, 80(8)
The American Museum, 87(146 octavo)
The American Negotiator, 77(33)
American Ornithology, 82(2 folio)
The American Register, 30(108)
The American Remembrancer, 13(522)
The American Senator, 13(516)
L'Amérique délivrée, 86(26)
Ames, Fisher, 87(242)
An Analysis of Antient Mythology, 62(55)
The Anatomy of Melancholy, 64(28)
The Ancient History of the Egyptians, Carthaginians, Assyrians, Babylonians . . . , 29(61)
Anderson, Adam, 77(1), 77(20), 79(5 quarto)
Anderson, Alexander, eng., 82(21), 86(44)
Annales de la Petite-Russie, 12(283)
Annales romaines, 13(14)
Annals of Commerce, Manufactures, Fisheries and Navigation, 79(5 quarto)
The Annual Register of World Events, 30(24)
Anquetil, Louis Pierre, 12(180), 23(48)
Anthing, Johann Friedrich, 31(337)
Anti-Jacobin; or, Weekly Examiner, 85(3)
The Antient Law-Merchant, 79(4 folio)
The Antient Right of the Commons of England, 56(7)
Anville, Jean Baptiste Bourguignon d', 39(1), 39(2), 39(14)
An Appeal to Impartial Posterity, 30(338)
Appianus, of Alexandria, 12(5)
Arbuthnot, John, 12(71)
Argou, Gabriel, 48(28)
Aristoteles, 62(5)
Aristotle's Ethics and Politics, 62(5)
Arrianus, Flavius, 12(89)
Ash, John, 67(7), 67(8)
Ashby, Matthew, 48(10)
Ashby and White; or, The Great Question, 48(10)
Ashe, Thomas, 37(10)
Ashley Cooper, Maurice, tr., 36(94)

Asiatic Society (Calcutta), 13(464)
Asiatick Researches, 13(464)
Assalini, Paolo, 84(32)
The Atlantic Neptune, 39(Desbarre's)
Athenae oxonienses, 34(67)
Atkyns, Sir Robert, 48(223)
Auckland, William Eden, baron, 56(90)
Aurora. General Advertiser, 93(*General Advertiser*)
Austin, William, ed., 91(121)
An Authentic Account of An Embassy from the King of Great Britain to the Emperor of China, 45(31)
Avaux, Claude de Mesmes, comte d', 21(67)
Avenia, 86(47)
Ayuni, Domenico Alberto, 48(198)

B

Babié de Bercenay, François, 35(345)
Baccaria, Cesare Bonesana, marchese di, 50(118)
Bache, Benjamin Franklin, 93(*General Advertiser*)
Bache's General Advertiser. See *The General Advertiser . . .* and *Aurora. General Advertiser*
Bacon, Francis, viscount St. Albans, 14(147), 87(50), 88(197)
Bacon, Matthew, 48(8), 49(149)
Bacon, Nathaniel, 49(16)
The Bankrupt Laws, 50(116). See also *A Compendious System of the Bankrupt Laws*
Banks, Sir Joseph, 41(14)
Barbeyrac, Jean, 56(1), 88(121); tr., 52(2), 54(24)
Baretti, Giuseppe Marc' Antonio, 68(13)
Barillon, Paul, 19(322)
Barlow, Joel, 85(2), 86(27)
Barr, tr., 82(5)
Barrow, Sir John, 38(82)
Barthélemy, Jean Jacques, 46(108)
Barton, Benjamin Smith, 15(422), 43(1)
Barton, William, 77(31)
Bartram, William, 37(56)
Bate, Julius, 68(9)
Bates, Ely, 62(29)
Bathurst, Richard, 92(249)

Bayard, Samuel, 49(284)
Bayle, Pierre, 14(46)
Beauclerk, Lady Diana (Spencer), illus., 85(1)
Beaumarchais, Pierre Augustin Caron de, ed., 92(66)
Beattie, James, 62(13), 62(15), 68(23)
Beaujour, Louis Auguste Félix, baron de, 77(29)
Beaumont, William, tr., 46(108)
Beawes, Wyndham, 78(1), 78(3 folio)
Beckmann, Johann, 88(319)
Bedingfield, Thomas, tr., 24(6)
Belknap, Jeremy, 15(374), 15(444)
Bellers, Fettiplace, 49(38)
Bellewe, Richard, comp., 54(40)
Bellin, Jacques Nicolas, 37(16)
Beloe, William, tr., 21(86)
Belsham, William, 14(44)
Benyovszky, Móric, gróf, 46(38)
Beresford, Benjamin, tr., 23(64)
Berthelson, Andreas, 68(20), 68(22)
Berthre de Bourniseaux, Pierre Victor Jean, 34(341)
Besenval, Pierre Victor, baron de, 25(350)
Besnier, Pierre, 68(3)
Bewick, Thomas, 82(21)
Bible, 11(1)
Bibliotheca Americana, 87(58)
Bibliotheca classica, 70(22)
Bibliotheque orientale, 14(61)
Biggs, James, 22(46)
Bijnkershoek, Cornelis van, 51(236), 88(156)
Binney, Horace, 49(67)
Biographia Britannica, 14(62)
Biographical Memoirs of Lord Viscount Nelson, 17(306)
Biographical Memoirs of the French Revolution, 12(178)
Bisset, Robert, 14(248), 14(307)
Black, John, tr., 21(430)
Black, Joseph, 85(46)
Black, William, 83(17)
Blackstone, Sir William, 49(1), 49(224), 49(228)
Blair, Hugh, 65(26)
Blair, John, 13(1)
Blair, William, 84(33)
Blane, Sir Gilbert, 83(16)
Blaquiere, Capt., tr., 31(272)

Blodget, Samuel, 71(82)
Bloomfield, Robert, 86(44)
Boccaccio, Giovanni, 85(1)
Bohun, William, 49(15)
Boileau, Daniel, tr., 28(44)
Bolingbroke, Henry Saint-John, viscount, 71(43)
Booth, George, tr., 14(4)
Borel, Pierre, 68(3)
Bossuet, Jacques Bénigne, 15(9)
Boswell, James, 14(311), 38(46)
The Botanic Garden, 86(23)
Boucher d'Argis, Antoine Gaspard, ed., 48(28)
Boudot, Pierre Jean, 22(21)
Bougainville, Louis Antoine, comte de, 37(37), 43(60)
Bougeant, Guillaume Hyacinth, 21(67)
Bourgoing, Jean François, baron de, 38(86)
Boyer, Abel, 68(16)
Bozman, John Leeds, 15(385)
Bracton, Henry de, 49(39)
Branagan, Thomas, 62(54), 86(47)
Brent, Nathanael, tr., 11(2)
A Brief Retrospect of the Eighteenth Century, 91(244)
Bristed, John, 71(35)
The British Cicero, 65(45)
The British Theatre, 86(60)
Brooke, Henry, 87(160)
Brooke, Sir Robert, 54(40)
Brookes, Richard, 37(10 octavo)
Brougham, Henry Peter, baron, 71(13)
Brown, Andrew, 93(*Brown's*)
Brown, Charles Brockden, tr., 47(59)
Brown, Thomas, surgeon, Musselburgh, 84(26)
Brown, William, 50(5)
Brown's Philadelphia Gazette. See *Federal Gazette, and Philadelphia Evening Post* and *The Philadelphia Gazette*
Browne, Arthur, 49(239)
Browne, Thomas, 65(45)
Bruce, James, 37(26)
Bruzen de La Martinière, Antoine Augustin, 27(199)
Bryant, Jacob, 62(55), 63(61)
Brydone, Patrick, 38(13)
Byron, John, 41(14)
Buffa, John, 38(99)

Buffon, Georges Louis Leclerc, comte de, 82(5)
Buffon's Natural History, 82(5)
Burgh, James, 62(4), 71(24)
Burke, Edmund, 15(454), 65(56), 87(55), 87(136); ed., 30(24)
Burke, William, 15(454)
Burlamaqui, Jean Jacques, 49(104)
Burn, Richard, ed., 49(1)
Burnet, Gilbert, tr., 87(162)
Burns, Robert, 86(35)
Burr, Aaron, 50(262), 50(263)
Burton, Robert, 64(28)
Büsching, Anton Friedrich, 37(5)
Butler, Charles, ed., 50(3), 50(156)
Bynkershoek, Cornelis van. *See* Bijkershoek, Cornelis van

C

Cà da Mosto, Alvise, supp. author, 50(42)
Caesar, Caius Julius, 18(7)
Caines, George, 78(3 octavo); reporter, 50(77)
Calepino, Ambrogio, 68(5)
Calvinus, Johannes, 50(14)
Campaigns of the Armies of France, 17(330)
Campbell, Thomas, 86(36)
Canning, George, 75(36)
Card, Henry, 16(281), 16(282)
Carew, George, of Lincoln's Inn, tr., 56(1)
Carey, Mathew, 13(522), 39(49); ed., 87(146 octavo)
Carey's American Pocket Atlas, 39(49)
Carpenter, Thomas, reporter, 13(516)
Carr, Sir John, 87(163)
Carteret, Philip, 41(14)
Carver, Jonathan, 39(50)
Cary, John, 38(4)
Cary's New Universal Atlas, 38(4)
Casaregi, Giuseppe Lorenzo Maria de, 50(42)
Case of King Charles the First, 24(43)
Caseneuve, Pierre de, 68(3)
Cases in Crown Law, 54(182)
Castéra, J., 33(279)
Cato and Laelius: or, Essays on Old-Age and Friendship, 63(16)
Catrou, François, 22(38)

Catteau-Calleville, Jean Pierre Guillaume, 16(259)
Cavallo, Tiberius, 82(24)
Cave, Edward, ed., 89(1)
Census of the United States for 1791 and 1800, 71(91)
Cervantes Saavedra, Miguel de, 87(150)
Chalmers, George, 51(272)
Chambers, Ephraim, 88(36)
Chaptal de Chanteloup, Jean Antoine Claude, comte d', 85(42)
Characteristicks of Men, Manners, Opinions, Times, 64(1 octavo)
Charbuy, François Nicolas, 13(15)
Charlevoix, Pierre François, 39(51)
Charnock, John, 17(306)
Chase, Samuel, defendant, 58(267)
Chastelain, Claude, 68(3)
Chaucer, Geoffrey, 85(1)
Chaussard, Pierre Jean Baptiste, 41(108)
Chavannes de la Giraudière, L— de, 86(26)
Chemistry Applied to Arts and Manufactures, 85(42)
The Chemical Catechism, 85(49)
Chénier, Louis de, 16(188)
Chesapeake and Delaware Canal Company, 91(325)
Child, Sir Josiah, 78(40)
Chipman, Nathaniel, 51(13)
Christian, Edward, ed., 49(224)
Christian Politics, 62(29)
Chronicles of England, France and the adjoining Countries, 19(Froissart's)
The Chronological Historian, 32(384)
The Chronology and History of the World, 13(1)
The Chronology of Antient Kingdoms Amended, 26(2 folio)
Cicero, Marcus Tullius, 63(16), 66(30), 66(32), 88(266)
Civil and Natural History of the Empire of China, 18(8)
The Civil Law in Its Natural Order, Together with the Publick Law, 51(10)
Clarendon, Edward Hyde, 1st earl of, 15(25)
*Clarendon's Parliamentary Chronicle,** 17(639)

109

Des Barres, Joseph Frederick Wallet, 39(Desbarre's)
Description of a Chart of Biography, 28(37)
Description of a New Chart of History, 28(36 duodecimo)
The Description of Greece, 27(78)
Des loix pénales, 51(282)
Desmaizeaux, Pierre, ed., 14(46)
Destutt de Tracy, Antoine Louis Claude, comte, 48(107)
De sublimitate, 67(37), 67(38)
Les devoirs de l'homme, et du citoien, 54(24)
D'Ewes, Sir Simonds, 18(89)
Díaz del Castillo, Bernal, 23(59)
Dibdin, Thomas Frognall, 69(21)
Dickinson, John, 72(56)
Dictionarium [octolingue], 68(5)
Dictionarium saxonico et gothico-latinum, 69(1 folio)
Dictionarium suethico-anglo-latinum, 68(23 quarto)
The Dictionary Historical and Critical of Mr. Peter Bayle, 14(46)
The Dictionary of Merchandise, and Nomenclature in All Languages, 78(7)
A Dictionary of the English Language, 69(10)
A Dictionary, Spanish and English, and English and Spanish, 68(13)
Dictionnaire de l'Académie françoise, 68(14)
Dictionnaire etymologique de la langue françoise, 68(3)
Dictionnaire françois-anglois et anglois-françois, 68(16)
Dictionnaire raisonné de diplomatique, 72(86)
Dictionnaire universel des sciences morale, economique, politique et diplomatique, 88(59)
Diderot, Denis, 88(1 folio)
A Digest of the Law Respecting County Elections, 53(245)
A Digest of the Laws of England, Comyns, 50(143); Cruise, 51(169)
A Digest of the Laws of the United States of America, 61(Herty)

The Dignity of Human Nature, 62(4)
Diodorus *Siculus*, 14(4)
Dionysius, of Halicarnassus, 31(5)
Discours sur l'art de négocier, 72(109)
Discourses on government, 75(1), 75(1 Same)
A Dissertation on the Freedom of Navigation and Maritime Commerce, 77(31)
Dissertation on the Gipseys, 20(340)
A Dissertation on the Numbers of Mankind, 76(37)
A Dissertation on the Prophecies, 63(48)
Dissertations on Man ... in answer to Mr. Malthus's "Essay on the Principle of Population," 73(15)
Dissertations on the English Language, 70(23)
Dobson, Mrs. Susannah (Dawson), ed. and tr., 18(314)
Dobson, Thomas, 88(1 quarto)
Documents Accompanying the Message of the President of the United States, 72(95)
Dodson, Michael, ed., 52(180)
Dogherty, Thomas, ed., 53(178)
Domat, Jean, 51(10)
Don Quixote, 87(150)
Douxménil, 26(60)
Dow, Alexander, tr., 18(285)
Le droit public de France, 56(15)
Drummond, William, tr., 86(28)
Dryden, John, 85(1)
Duane, William, 74(96), 80(7), 80(8), 93(*General Advertiser*)
Dubois, Edward, 87(163)
Du cotonnier et da sa culture, 81(8)
Dufief, Nicolas Gouin, 69(16)
Du Halde, Jean Baptiste, 18(8)
Dunbar, James, 63(30)
Duncan, William, tr., 18(7)
Dunlap, John, 93(*Dunlap's*)
Dunlap and Claypoole's Daily American Advertiser, 93(*Claypoole's*)
Dunlap's Daily American Advertiser, 93(*Dunlap's*)
Dunn, Samuel, 39(4)
Dunton, John, supposed author, 75(38)
Du Penceau, Peter Stephen, tr., 51(236)
Durnford, Charles, 57(44)

E

East, Sir Edward Hyde, 52(184), 57(44)
Ebers, Johann, 69(1 octavo)
An Ecclesiastical History, Antient and Modern, 11(33)
Economica, 71(82)
The Edinburgh Review, 66(1)
Edwards, Bryan, 19(48)
The Elements and Practice of Rigging, 80(10)
Elements of Chemistry, 84(41)
Elements of Galvanism, 82(22)
Elements of General History, 24(69)
Elements of Moral Science, 62(13)
Elements of the History of France, 26(2 duodecimo)
Elements of the Law Relating to Insurances, 55(219)
Ellicott, Andrew, 40(42)
The Eloquence of the British Senate, Being A Selection of the Best Speeches, 66(48)
Elphinston, James, tr., 15(9)
Elsynge, Henry, 52(6)
Emérigon, Balthazard Marie, 56(26)
Emlyn, Sollom, ed., 48(19)
Encyclopedia; or, A Dictionary of Arts, Sciences, and Miscellaneous Literature, 88(1 quarto)
Encyclopédie; ou, Dictionnaire raisonné des sciences, des arts, et des métiers, 88(1 folio)
An English and Danish Dictionary, 68(20), 68(22)
The English Works of Sir Henry Spelman, 57(43)
An Enquiry Concerning Political Justice, and Its Influence on General Virtue and Happiness, 72(16)
An Enquiry into the Foundation and History of the Law of Nations, 59(97)
An Enquiry into the Law Merchant of the United States, 78(3 octavo)
Ensor, George, 63(18)
Epaminondas on the Government of the Territory of Columbia, 72(49)
Ἔπεα πτεροεντα. or, The Diversions of Purley . . . , 69(18)
Epistles, Odes, and Other Poems, 85(19)
An Epitome of Chemistry, 85(50)
Erdbeschreibung und geschichte von Amerika, 40(1)
Espinasse, Isaac, ed., 52(73)
Espriella, Don Manuel Alvarez. *See* Southey, Robert
Esprit de l'histoire générale de l'Europe, 19(502)
L'esprit de la ligue, ou Histoire politique des troubles de France, 23(48)
An Essay on Crimes and Punishment, 50(118)
An Essay on Military Law, 58(235)
Essay on National Pride, 63(50)
An Essay on Naval Tactics, 80(1)
An Essay on Privateers, Captures, and . . . Recaptures, 55(217)
Essay on the Causes of the Variety of Complexion and Figure, 82(37)
An Essay on the History of Civil Society, 63(23)
An Essay on the Nature and Immutability of Truth, 62(15)
An Essay on the Principle of Population, 79(9)
An Essay on the True Principles of Executive Power in Great States, 74(71)
An Essay on Wool, 81(7)
Essay Upon the Law of Contracts and Agreements, 56(238)
Essays, Mathematical and Physical, 91(324)
Essays on Philosophical Subjects, 82(38)
Essays on Physiognomy, 90(153)
Essays on the History of Mankind in Rude and Cultivated Ages, 63(30)
Essays on the Intellectual and Active Powers of Man, 64(2)
Essays on the Mind and its Several Faculties, 63(26)
Essays, Political, Economical, and Philosophical, 91(246)
Estrades, Godefroi Louis, comte d', 73(104)
Etymologicon Linguae, 70(7)
Eulogies and Orations on the Life and Death of General George Washington, 66(52)
European Commerce, 79(14)
An Examination of the British Doctrine which subjects to Capture a Neutral Trade, 71(59)
An Examination of the Conduct of Great Britain Respecting Neutrals,

71(90)
The Expedition of Cyrus into Persia, 36(91)
An Exposition of Christian Doctrine, 62(39)
Extracts from the Votes and Proceedings of the American Continental Congress, 72(92)

F

Faber, George Stanley, 63(48)
The Fable of the Bees, 86(32)
The Fables of John Dryden, 85(1)
Facts and Observations relative to ... the Pestilential Fever, 84(31)
Fairfax, Ferdinando, 66(54)
The Farmer's Boy, 86(44)
Farneworth, Ellis, tr., 18(19), 90(220)
Fawcett, Sir William, tr., 80(2)
Federal Gazette, and Philadelphia Evening Post, 93(*Brown's*)
The Federalist, 76(68), 76(97)
Fell, Ralph, 40(69)
Fenno, John Ward, 93(*Gazette*)
Ferguson, Adam, 19(101), 63(23)
Ferguson, James, 41(2 quarto), 41(3)
Fêtes et courtisanes de la Grece, 41(108)
Fielding, Henry, 89(94)
Fielding, Sarah, tr., 36(96)
Filangieri, Gaetano, 52(285)
Firishtah, Muhammad Kāsim Hindū Shāh, Astarābādī, 18(285)
The First Part of the Institutes of the Laws of England, 50(3), 50(156)
Fitzherbert, Sir Anthony, 54(36)
The Florentine Historie, 24(6)
The Flower and the Leaf, 85(1)
Foedera, 28(36 folio)
Foley, Robert, 48(8)
The Fool of Quality, 87(160)
Forbes, Sir William, bart., 19(319)
Forensic Eloquence, 66(39)
Forster, John Reinhold, 38(102), 40(55); tr., 37(37)
Foster, Sir Michael, 52(180)
Fox, Charles James, 19(322)
France. Commissaires sur les possessions et les droits de la Grand-Bre-

tagne et de la France en Amérique, 24(72)
Francisco de Miranda, Don, 22(46)
Francklin, Thomas, ed., 92(1)
Franklin, Benjamin, 12(383), 89(235), 89(339)
Fraser, Simon, 52(244)
The Frederician Code, 52(250)
Freneau, Philip Morin, 86(40)
Friedrich II, king of Prussia, 26(6), 89(207)
Froissart, Jean, 19(Froissart's)
Fulton, Robert, 89(323)

G

Gales, Joseph, Jr., 93(*National Intelligencer*)
Gallatin, Albert, 73(31), 89(326)
Gaudin, Alexis, 14(46)
Gazette de Leyde. See *Journal Politique*
Gazette of the United States & Daily Advertiser, 93(*Gazette*)
Gazetteer of France, 41(2 duodecimo)
The Gazetteer of Scotland, 41(12)
Gee, Joshua, 78(39)
A General Abridgment of Cases in Equity, 48(8)
A General Abridgment of Law and Equity, 59(119)
General Account of Miranda's Expedition, 13(503)
The General Advertiser and Political, Commercial and Literary Journal, 93(*General Advertiser*)
A General Collection of the Best and Most Interesting Voyages and Travels, 43(46)
The General Gazetteer, 37(10 octavo)
A General History of Connecticut, 12(10)
The General History of Polybius, 20(3 quarto)
A General History of Quadrupeds, 82(21)
A General History of the British Empire in America, 35(396)
The General History of the Vast Continent and Islands of America,

114

Hederich, Benjamin, 69(8)
Héloïse, 24(62)
Helvétius, Claude Adrien, 63(24), 63(26)
Helwig, Christoph, 20(3 folio)
Henault, Charles Jean François, 22(19), 22(21)
Henderson, Thomas, Jr., 93(*Raleigh Star*)
Hening, William W., 53(65)
Henry, Alexander, 42(81)
Henry, David, ed., 89(1)
Henry, Robert, 21(120)
Henry, William, 85(50)
Henshaw, Thomas, ed., 70(7)
Herbelot de Molainville, Barthélemy d', 14(61)
Herbert, Edward Herbert, baron, 20(16)
Heriot, George, 21(395)
Hermes; or, A Philosophical Inquiry Concerning Universal Grammar, 69(25)
Herodotus, 21(86)
Herrera y Tordesillas, Antonio, 21(434)
Herschel, Sir William, 41(2 quarto)
Herty, Thomas, 61(Herty's—U.S.)
Hertzberg, Ewald Friedrich, graf von, 75(83)
Heywood, Samuel, 53(245)
Hints for "A Rygbye Merrie and Conceitede" Tour, 87(163)
Hints on the National Bankruptcy of Britain, 71(35)
Histoire des guerres et des negociations que precederent le Traite de Westphalie, 21(67)
L'histoire du monde, 81(1 folio)
Histoire generale de l'empire du Mogul, 22(38)
Histoire raisonnée du commerce de la Russie, 78(37)
An Historical Account of the Black Empire of Hayti, 29(60)
Historical and Chronological Deduction of the Origin of Commerce, 77(1), 77(20)
Historical and Chronological Theatre of Christopher Helvicus, 20(3 folio)
Historical and Political Discourse of the Laws and Government of England, 49(16)

Historical and Political Memoirs of the Reign of Lewis XVI, 31(169)
An Historical and Practical Essay on the Culture and Commerce of Tobacco, 81(6)
Historical Collections: or, An Exact Account of the Proceedings of the Four Last Parliaments of Q. Elizabeth, 32(73)
Historical Collections of Private Passages of State, 28(17)
An Historical Disquisition concerning the Knowledge which the Ancients Had of India, 29(292)
An Historical Dissertation, 32(505)
The Historical Library of Diodorus the Sicilian, 14(4)
The Historical Register, 30(1)
Historical Review of the Administration of Mr. Necker, 27(342)
An Historical Review of the Constitution and Government of Pennsylvania, 12(383)
An Historical Review of the State of Ireland, 27(252)
An Historical Sketch of Medicine and Surgery, 83(17)
An Historical Sketch of the Civil War in the Vendée, 34(341)
An Historical View of the English Government, 24(264)
The History and Adventures of the Renowned Don Quixote, 87(150)
The History, Civil and Commercial, of the British Colonies in the West Indies, 19(48)
History of Alexander's Expedition, 12(89)
The History of America, Robertson, 29(28), 30(388)
The History of Ancient Greece, 19(74)
The History of Canada, 21(395)
The History of Cataline's Conspiracy, 31(9)
The History of Charles the XIIth, King of Sweden, 34(161)
History of Don Francisco de Miranda's Attempt to Effect a Revolution in South America, 22(46)
The History of England, Hume, 20(32), 21(234)
The History of England, Rapin-Thoy-

ras, 28(11)

The History of Great Britain, Belsham, 14(44)

The History of Great Britain, Henry, 21(120)

The History of Greece, 24(81)

The History of Helvetia, 27(268)

The History of Henry, Earl of Morland. See *The Fool of Quality*

The History of Hindostan, 18(285)

A History of Inventions and Discoveries, 88(319)

History of Ireland, Gordon, 20(257)

History of Ireland, Leland, 23(40)

The History of Italy, 20(131)

The History of Louisiana, or of the Western parts of Virginia and Carolina, 18(416)

The History of Mexico, 16(23)

The History of Modern Europe, 16(119), 29(112)

The History of New-England, 27(372)

The History of New Hampshire, 15(374)

A History of New York, 87(158)

History of Poland, 21(276)

The History of Political Transactions, 75(40)

The History of Printing in America, 92(162)

History of Russia, 33(277)

History of Scotland, 29(30)

The History of the American Revolution, 30(407)

The History of the Anglo-Saxons, 33(261)

History of the British Expedition to Egypt, 35(323)

The History of the British Plantations in America, 22(57)

History of the Campaigns of Count Alexander Suworow Rymnikski, 31(337)

The History of the Civil Wars of France, 18(19)

The History of the Colony of Massachusetts-Bay, 21(358). See also *Continuation of the History of the Province of Massachusetts Bay*

The History of the Colony of Nova-Caesaria, or New Jersey, 32(382)

The History of the Conquest of Mexico, 18(10)

The History of the Council of Trent, 11(2)

The History of the Decline and Fall of the Roman Empire, 19(13)

A History of the Early Part of the Reign of James the Second, 19(322)

History of the English Law, 57(108)

The History of the First Discovery and Settlement of Virginia, 32(387)

The History of the Five Indian Nations of Canada, 17(398)

A History of the Law of Shipping, 57(214)

History of the Life and Reign of Philip, King of Macedon, 23(93)

The History of the Life of Gustavus Adolphus, King of Sweden, 20(50)

History of the Life of Henry the Second, 23(141)

The History of the Life of Marcus Tullius Cicero, 24(98)

History of the Mission of the United Brethren among the Indians in North America, 42(117)

The History of the Origin, Progress, and Termination of the American War, 31(62)

History of the Original Constitution of Parliaments, 56(222)

The History of the Peloponnesian War, 32(1)

The History of the Pleas of the Crown, 53(178)

History of the Principal Events of the Reign of Frederic William II, 31(294)

The History of the Progress and Termination of the Roman Republic, 19(101)

The History of the Province of New York, 32(381)

The History of the Public Revenue, 75(4 quarto), 75(4 Same)

History of the Punick, Syrian, Parthian, Mithridatick, Illyrian, Spanish and Hannibalic Wars, 12(5)

The History of the Rebellion and Civil Wars in England begun in the year 1641, 15(25)

The History of the Reign of Emperor Charles V, 29(25)

History of the Reign of George III, 14(248)

118

Irving, Washington, 87(158)

J

Jackson, James Grey, 42(9)
Jackson, John, d. 1807, 42(94), 78(35)
Jackson, Richard, 12(383)
Jackson, Robert, 84(30)
Jacob, Giles, 53(22)
Jarrold, Thomas, 73(15)
Jault, Auguste François, ed., 68(3)
Jeannin, Pierre, 73(110)
Jefferson, Thomas, 22(386). *See also*
  U.S. President, 1801–1809 (Jefferson)
Jefferys, Thomas, 42(5 folio)
Jeffrey, Francis Jeffrey, lord, ed., 66(1)
Johnes, Thomas, tr., 19(Froissart's)
Johnson, J., tr., 34(161)
Johnson, Samuel, 14(311), 38(46),
  46(25), 69(10), 90(58), 92(149)
Johnson, William, 53(44), 53(46),
  53(51)
Johnston, William, ed., 93(271); tr.,
  38(102), 88(319)
Jones, Anna Maria (Shipley) lady, ed.,
  90(42)
Jones, Calvin, 93(*Raleigh Star*)
Jones, John, 1766?–1827, 64(40)
Jones, Stephen, 21(276)
Jones, Sir William, 90(42), 90(174)
Josephus, Flavius, 35(490)
The Journal of a Tour to the Hebrides,
  38(46)
Journal of A Voyage to North America, 39(51)
*A Journal of Natural Philosophy,
  Chemistry, and the Arts*, 82(2 quarto)
A Journal of Travels in England,
  45(70)
Journal Politique, 90(151)
*The Journals of All the Parliaments
  during the Reign of Queen Elizabeth*, 18(89)
Journals of Congress (1777–1788),
  61(Journals)
Journals of the House of Commons,
  22(108)
Journals of the House of Lords, 22(74)
Journals of Travels in parts of the Late

*Austrian Low Countries, France, the
  Pays de Vaud, and Tuscany*, 43(74)
Journey from India, towards England in . . . 1797, 42(94)
*A Journey from Prince of Wales's Fort,
  in Hudson's Bay, to the Northern
  Ocean*, 42(58)
*A Journey, Made in the Summer of
  1794*, 44(47)
The Judge, 87(145)
*Judgment of Whole Kingdoms and
  Nations*, 75(38)
Junius, *pseud.*, 90(119)
Jura Anglorum, 56(256)
*The Jurisdiction of the Lords House,
  or Parliament, Considered according to Antient Records*, 53(41)
Jus Parliamentarium, 56(18)
Justamon, John Obediah, tr., 30(446)
Justinian's Institutions, 53(26)
Juvenalis, Decimus Junius, 85(15),
  85(16)

K

Kames, Henry Home, lord, 53(254)
Kauffman, C. H., 78(7)
Keating, Maurice, tr., 23(59)
Keith, Sir William, 22(57)
Kennett, Basil, tr., 56(1)
Kenrick, W. S., tr., 34(161)
Kerr, Robert, tr., 84(41)
*A Key to the Classical Pronunciation
  of Greek, Latin, and Scripture*, 70(10)
Kippis, Andrew, ed., 14(62), 30(70),
  30(85)
Kirby, Ephraim, reporter, 54(86)
Kirwan, Richard, 81(10), 82(4)
Knickerbocker, Diedrich. *See* Irving,
  Washington
Knox, Hugh, 64(51)
Knox, John, supposed author, 41(1),
  41(2 quarto), 41(3)
*Koran, commonly called the Alcoran
  of Mohammed*, 65(31)
Kościuszko, Tadeusz Andrzej Bonawentura, 80(15)
Kotzebue, August Friedrich Ferdinand von, 23(64), 42(5 duodecimo)

L

Labillardière, Jacques Julien Houton de, 42(40)

Lacombe, Jacques, 22(19), 22(28)

Lacroix, Irenée Amelot de, 80(17), 80(21)

Laing, Malcolm, ed., 21(120)

Lambert, William, comp., 61(Lambert's)

Lancaster, Joseph, 70(28)

The Lancasterian System of Education, 70(28)

Langhorne, John, 23(61), 27(106)

Langhorne, William, 27(106)

Langworthy, Edward, 25(422)

Lantier, Étienne François de, 47(105)

Lapérouse, Jean François de Galaup, comte de, 44(37)

La Platière, Sulpice Imbert, comte de, 35(345)

La Rouchefoucauld, François, duc de, 91(125)

Lasteyrie du Saillant, Charles Philibert, comte de, 81(8)

Latrobe, Benjamin, 62(39)

LaTrobe, Christian Ignatius, tr., 42(117)

Latude, Jean Henri Masers de, 24(70)

Lauderdale, James Maitland, 8th earl of, 73(20)

Lavater, Johann Caspar, 90(153)

Lavoisier, Antoine Laurent, 84(41)

The Law-Dictionary, 53(22)

The Law of Nations, 59(93), 59(94), 59(95)

The Law of Nature and Nations, 56(1)

Laws and Ordinances of the City of New York, 55(89)

Laws of individual states. *See* Acts and laws of individual states

The Laws of the United States of America, 61(Laws of U.S.)

Laws, Treaties, and other Documents, Having Operation and Respect to the Public Lands, 61(Public Lands)

Leach, Thomas, ed., 53(174), 54(182)

Le Clerc, Jean, 28(36 folio)

Lecteur françois: ou, Receuil de pièces ... pour servir à perfectionner les jeunes gens dans la lecture, 90(124)

Lectures on History, 28(514), 34(1 duodecimo)

Lectures on Law. See The Works of the Honorable James Wilson

Lectures on Rhetoric and Belles Lettres, 65(26)

Lectures on Rhetoric and Oratory, 65(50)

Lectures on the Constitution, 58(249)

Lectures on the Elements of Chemistry, 85(46)

Lectures on the Elements of Commerce, Politics, and Finances, 79(18)

Le Duchat, Jacob, 87(146)

Lee, Charles, 25(442)

Lee, Richard, 54(216)

Leeuwen, Simon van, ed., 50(4)

Le Fèvre de La Boderie, Antoine, 13(53)

Leland, Thomas, 23(93), 40(23); tr., 67(34)

Lempriere, John, 23(486), 70(22)

Lempriere, William, 84(27)

Lenclos, Anne, called Ninon de, 26(60)

Lenglet Dufresnoy, Nicolas, 33(51)

Leonidas, A Poem, 86(45)

Le Page du Pratz, 18(416)

Letter from the Secretary of State to Mr. Monroe, on the subject of the Attack on the Chesapeake, 75(36)

A Letter in Reply to the Report of the Surgeons of the Vaccine Institution, 84(26)

Letters and Correspondence ... of Henry St. John, Bolingbroke, 71(43)

Letters and Reflections of the Austrian Field-Marshall Prince de Ligne, 28(44)

Letters ... between M. de St. Evremond and Mr. Waller, 23(61)

Letters Concerning the Spanish Nation, 16(58)

Letters from England, 19(39)

Letters from Scandinavia, 23(343)

The Letters of Junius Complete, 90(119)

The Letters of Pliny the Consul, 91(269)

Lettres et negociations entre M. Jean de Witt, 73(99)

Lettres, memoires, et negociations de monsieur le comte d'Estrades, 73(104)

Lettsom, John Coakley, 39(50)

Le Vaillant, François, 47(20)

Lexicon Iuridicum, 50(14)

Lexicon manuale graecum, 69(8)

Mitford, William, 24(81)
Modern Geography, 43(1)
Modus tenendi Parliamentum, 53(9)
Molina, Juan Ignacio, 25(428)
Molloy, Charles, 55(212)
Monroe, James, 71(59), 73(60), 75(36)
Montefiore, Joshua, 79(4 octavo)
Montesquieu, Charles Louis de Secondat, 55(106)
Monthly Intelligencer. See *Gentleman's Magazine*
Monthly Literary Review. See *The Monthly Review*
The Monthly Review, 67(14)
Montucla, Jean Étienne, ed., 82(27)
Monuments of Washington's Patriotism, 35(405)
Moore, John, 92(167)
Moore, Thomas, 85(19)
The Moral and Religious Miscellany, 64(51)
Moral Tales, 87(155)
More, Sir Thomas, 87(162)
Moreau de Saint Méry, Médéric Louis Élie, 45(17)
Moréri, Louis, 15(69), 18(51)
Morgan, William, ed., 74(22)
Morse, Jedidiah, 26(45), 42(11); comp., 43(11)
Mortimer, Thomas, 79(5 folio), 79(18); ed., 78(1), 78(3 folio); tr., 74(53)
Moseley, Benjamin, 84(23)
Mosheim, Johann Lorenz, 11(33)
The Most Remarkable Year in the Life of Augustus von Kotzebue, 23(64)
Moultrie, William, 25(393)
Moyle, Walter, ed. & tr., 78(9)
Muirhead, Lockhart, 43(74)
Mulgrave, Henry Phipps, 1st earl of, 71(59)
Munford, William, 53(65)
Murdoch, Patrick, tr., 37(5)
Murphy, Arthur, 89(94), 90(58); tr., 24(9)
Murray, Lindley, 90(124)
My Pocket Book, 87(163)
A Mythological, Etymological, and Historical Dictionary, 63(61)

N

The National Intelligencer, 93(*National Intelligencer*)
The Natural and Civil History of Vermont, 35(377), 35(379)
The Naval Surgeon, 83(18)
Naylor, Francis Hare, 27(268)
Neal, Daniel, 27(372)
Neale, Adam, tr., 84(32)
Necker, Jacques, 27(342), 74(53), 74(71)
Necker, Karl Friedrich, 72(93)
Neef, Joseph, 70(27)
Les negotiations de monsieur le president Ieannin, 73(110)
Neutral Rights, 74(89)
A New Abridgment of the Law, 49(149)
A New and Accurate History of South America, 30(433)
The New and Complete Dictionary of the English Language, 67(7), 67(8)
A New and Complete Dictionary of Trade and Commerce, 79(5 folio)
A New and Complete System of Geography, 44(3)
A New and General Biographical Dictionary, 15(471)
The New Annual Register, 30(70), 30(85)
A New Atlas of the Mundane System, 39(4)
A new Discourse of Trade, 78(40)
The New England Quarterly Magazine, 91(65)
New Hampshire. Laws, statutes, etc., 60(N.H. laws)
New Jersey. Laws, statutes, etc., 60(N.J. laws)
New Literary Journal. See *The Monthly Review*
A New System of Geography, 37(5)
A New System of Husbandry, 81(5)
A New System of Modern Geography, 41(1), 41(2 quarto), 41(3)
A New System, or, An Analysis of Antient Mythology, 62(55)
Newton, Sir Isaac, 26(2 folio)
A New Universal and Pronouncing Dictionary, 69(16)
The New Universal Gazetteer, 39(7)
New Views of the Origin of the Tribes

Sanderson, Robert, comp., 28(36 folio)
Sarpi, Paolo, 11(2)
The Satires of Decimus Junius Juvenalis, 85(15), 85(16)
The Satires of Persius, 86(28)
Saxe, Maurice, comte de, 80(2)
Scherer, Jean-Benoît, 12(283), 78(37)
Schiller, Johann Christoph Friedrich von, 31(272)
Schlegel, Johan Frederik Vilhelm, 74(89)
La scienza della legislazione, 52(285)
Scobell, Henry, 57(13)
Scott, Sir Walter, 86(37)
The Secret History of the Court and Cabinet of St. Cloud, 31(334)
Ségur, Louis Philippe, comte de, 31(294)
Selden, John, 49(16), 92(41)
A Selection of Pleadings in Civil Actions, 57(194)
A Selection of the Most Admired Speeches in the English Language, 65(45)
A Selection of the Patriotic Addresses, to the President of the United States, 91(121)
Selfridge, Thomas Oliver, 58(269)
Selkirk, Thomas Douglas, 5th earl of, 76(88)
Serenius, Jakob, 68(23 quarto)
Several Essays in Political Arithmetick, 74(79)
Sévigné, Charles, marquis de, 26(60)
Shaftesbury, Anthony Ashley Cooper, 3d earl of, 64(1 octavo)
Shakespeare, William, 86(48)
Sheffield, John Baker Holroyd, 1st earl of, 79(26), 89(224)
Sheridan, Thomas, 92(70)
Sherman, John, H., 13(503)
The Ship-master's Assistant, 81(23)
Sidney, Algernon, 75(1), 75(Same)
Silliman, Benjamin, 45(70)
Simon de Val-Hébert, H. P., 68(3)
Sinclair, Sir John, 75(4 quarto),75(4 Same), 83(19)
Sketch of a Plan and Method of Education, 70(27)
A Sketch of the Finances of the United States, 73(31)

A Sketch of the History of Maryland, 15(385)
Sketches of Trials in Ireland for High Treason, 66(39)
Skinner, Joseph, comp. & tr., 27(60)
Skinner, Stephen, 70(7)
Skinner, Thomas, 25(321)
Sleidanus, Johannes, 13(18)
Smart, Christopher, comp., 46(25)
Smellie, William, 82(1 quarto)
Smirnove, James, tr., 28(41), 44(16 quarto)
Smith, Adam, 65(5), 75(4 octavo), 75(7), 82(38)
Smith, Elihu Hubbard, ed., 83(1), 91(Mitchill)
Smith, Samuel Harrison, 93(*National Intelligencer*); reporter, 58(267)
Smith, Samuel Stanhope, 82(37)
Smith, Sydney, ed., 66(1)
Smith, Sir Thomas, 51(12)
Smith, William, 1711–1787, tr., 67(37)
Smith, William, 1728–1793, 32(381)
Smith, William Stephens, 58(264)
Smollett, Tobias George, 92(167); ed. & tr., 87(150), 92(1)
Society for the Promotion of Agriculture, Arts, and Manufactures. *See* Society for the Promotion of Useful Arts
Society for the Promotion of Useful Arts, 81(3)
The Soldier's Friend, 84(33)
Solis y Rivadeneyra, Antonio de, 18(10)
Sollom, Emlyn, 53(178)
Somers, John Somers, baron, supposed author, 75(38)
Sommerville, Thomas, 75(40)
Sonnini de Manoncourt, Charles Nicolas Sigisbert, 45(36), 45(114), 47(112)
Sotheby, William, tr., 85(18)
Soulavie, Jean Louis Giraud, 31(169)
Souquet de Latour, Guillaume Jean François, 86(33)
South Carolina. Laws, statutes, etc., 61(S.C. laws)
Southey, Robert, 19(39)
Spallanzani, Lazzaro, 45(89)
Spangenberg, August Gottlieb, 62(39)
The Spectator, 92(249)

130

Index to Places of Publication

49(38), 49(39), 49(104), 49(149), 49(224), 49(239), 50(3), 50(5), 50(37), 50(116), 50(118), 50(143), 50(156), 51(10), 51(11), 51(12), 51(272), 52(2), 52(6), 52(14), 52(27), 52(180), 52(244), 53(9), 53(22), 53(26), 53(32), 53(41), 53(174), 53(178), 54(36), 54(40), 54(181), 54(182), 54(216), 54(241), 54(276), 55(106), 55(212), 55(217), 55(218), 55(233), 56(1), 56(7), 56(18), 56(30), 56(90), 56(222), 57(8), 57(12), 57(13), 57(17), 57(43), 57(44), 57(80), 57(108), 57(214), 58(1 quarto), 58(6), 58(235), 59(93), 59(94), 59(97), 59(100), 59(119), 59(186), 59(271), 60(252), 62(4), 62(5), 62(15), 62(29), 62(55), 63(16), 63(18), 63(20), 63(24), 63(26), 63(30), 63(48), 63(61), 64(1 quarto), 64(7), 64(28), 64(40), 64(41), 65(5), 65(25), 65(26), 65(31), 66(30), 66(32), 66(55), 67(7), 67(8), 67(24), 67(34), 67(37), 67(41), 68(9), 68(12), 68(13), 68(20), 68(22), 68(23), 69(1 folio), 69(8), 69(10), 69(21), 69(25), 70(6), 70(7), 70(12), 70(20), 70(27), 71(21), 71(24), 71(34), 71(43), 71(47), 71(94), 72(18), 72(41), 72(93), 73(15), 74(22), 74(53), 74(71), 74(79), 74(89), 75(1), 75(2), 75(4 octavo), 75(4 quarto), 75(30), 75(38), 76(37), 76(39), 76(50), 76(88), 77(1), 77(29), 77(30), 77(33), 77(34), 78(3 folio), 78(9), 78(39), 78(40), 79(1), 79(4 folio), 79(5 folio), 79(5 quarto), 79(9), 79(18), 79(26), 80(2), 80(10), 80(21), 81(6), 81(7), 81(23), 82(2 quarto), 82(4), 82(5), 82(22), 82(24), 82(27), 82(31), 82(36), 83(16), 83(17), 83(18), 84(23), 84(24), 84(25), 84(27), 84(30), 84(33), 85(1), 85(3), 85(4), 85(7), 85(9), 85(15), 85(18), 85(42), 86(20), 86(28), 86(29), 86(31), 86(32), 86(39), 86(45), 86(48), 86(60), 86(80), 86(92), 87(50), 87(145), 87(146), 87(155), 87(158), 87(162), 88(59), 88(197), 88(266), 88(319), 89(1), 89(94), 89(207), 89(323), 89(339), 90(39), 90(42), 90(58), 90(119), 90(153), 90(174), 90(188), 90(220), 91(125), 91(246), 91(269), 91(276), 91(295), 92(1), 92(41), 92(70), 92(109), 92(140), 92(167), 92(231), 92(249), 93(271), 92(288)

Oxford, 15(25)

IRELAND

Dublin, 20(324), 24(81), 28(41), 30(407), 35(7), 37(56), 40(55), 42(58), 43(93), 44(95), 51(253), 53(245), 56(256), 59(246), 70(22), 72(16), 75(4 Same), 75(40), 77(20), 78(1), 82(38), 86(24), 86(25), 87(150), 88(36)

SCOTLAND

Edinburgh, 22(318), 27(399), 29(28), 29(175), 37(26), 41(12), 52(250), 55(219), 62(13), 64(2), 64(12), 66(1), 68(11), 71(13), 73(20), 78(8), 80(1), 82(1 quarto), 83(19), 84(29), 84(36)

The Netherlands

Amsterdam, 50(4), 54(24), 67(38), 73(99), 76(L'Ambassadeur), 86(26), 88(121)

The Hague, 22(38), 28(36 folio)

Leiden, 50(4), 54(18), 88(156), 90(151)

Maastricht, 14(61)

Sweden

Stockholm, 68(23 quarto)

Switzerland

Basel, 63(23), 89(224)

Geneva, 50(14), 56(15)

United States

CONNECTICUT

Hartford, 32(45), 33(353), 51(85), 52(73), 75(7)

Litchfield, 54(86)

Middletown, 15(335), 25(428)

New Haven, 91(324)

New London, 60(Conn. laws)

Windham, 57(91)

DELAWARE

Wilmington, 72(56)

DISTRICT OF COLUMBIA

Georgetown, 72(49), 93(*Washington Federalist*)

Washington, 50(263), 57(265), 58(267), 61(Herty's-U.S.),

135

61(Lambert's), 61(Public Lands), 71(82), 71(91), 72(95), 73(62), 73(66), 74(96), 75(36), 89(326), 93(*National Intelligencer*)

GEORGIA
Savannah, 61(Ga. laws)

MAINE
Portland, 58(249)

MARYLAND
Annapolis, 61(Md. laws)
Baltimore, 14(248), 15(385), 23(61), 44(118), 61(Herty), 61(Md. laws), 66(39), 83(14), 86(36), 87(160)

MASSACHUSETTS
Boston, 14(311), 15(444), 17(330), 22(46), 25(356), 25(440), 35(409), 49(1), 55(220), 58(269), 60(Mass. laws), 66(52), 70(23), 80(17), 83(14), 84(35), 86(37), 87(136), 87(242), 90(37), 90(115), 91(65), 91(121)
Cambridge, 17(359), 21(370), 65(50)
Charlestown, 26(45)
Northampton, 59(75), 59(95)
Salem, 57(194)
Worcester, 92(162)

NEW HAMPSHIRE
Dover, 60(N.H. laws)
Portsmouth, 60(N.H. laws)
Walpole, 35(377), 56(238)

NEW JERSEY
Burlington, 32(382), 60(N.J. laws)
New Brunswick, 60(N.J. laws), 82(37)
Trenton, 30(389), 60(N.J. laws)

NEW YORK
Albany, 60(N.Y. laws), 74(75), 81(3)
Flatbush, 53(65), 77(77)
New York, 13(62), 13(503), 17(306), 17(504), 17(645), 19(39), 21(430), 23(64), 23(486), 24(62), 24(260), 25(393), 26(443), 27(320), 30(406), 40(78), 40(105), 42(81), 44(3), 44(15), 45(70), 48(198), 49(284), 50(68), 50(77), 51(58), 51(169), 53(44), 53(46), 53(51), 55(89), 58(264), 60(N.Y. laws), 61(Journals), 63(43), 63(50), 66(32), 66(48), 68(26), 69(Johnson's), 70(28), 71(35), 73(31), 75(1 Same), 76(32), 76(68), 76(97), 78(3 octavo), 78(35), 80(15), 82(21), 82(37), 83(1), 83(38), 84(32), 84(34), 84(41),

86(23), 86(35), 86(44), 87(158), 87(163), 88(322), 89(166), 90(124), 91(Mitchill), 91(244), 93(*Gazette*)

NORTH CAROLINA
Edenton, 61(N.C. laws)
Newbern, 56(255), 61(N.C. laws)
Raleigh, 93(*Raleigh Star*)

PENNSYLVANIA
Lancaster, 58(270)
Philadelphia, 11(1), 11(33), 13(516), 13(522), 15(374), 15(422), 16(119), 17(420), 19(319), 19(322), 25(400), 26(42), 26(60), 27(252), 28(44), 28(514), 29(299), 30(388), 30(463), 31(334), 33(279), 33(309), 34(1 duodecimo), 34(326), 35(64), 35(323), 35(405), 38(82), 39(49), 39(84), 40(42), 41(3), 42(9), 43(1), 43(46), 44(14), 44(98), 44(118), 45(17), 46(25), 47(59), 48(107), 48(191), 49(67), 49(228), 50(262), 51(58), 51(61), 51(236), 52(184), 53(195), 55(101), 56(83), 58(257), 60(279), 61(Pa. laws), 61(S.C. laws), 62(52), 62(54), 64(51), 65(45), 65(46), 65(56), 69(16), 69(18), 69(29), 70(10), 70(27), 71(30), 71(59), 71(90), 72(57), 72(92), 73(60), 73(63), 74(73), 74(76), 76(33), 76(52), 76(66), 77(31), 78(7), 79(4 octavo), 79(14), 79(61), 80(5), 80(7), 80(8), 80(14), 81(1 octavo), 81(5), 81(10), 82(1 octavo), 82(2 folio), 83(14), 83(15), 83(39), 84(31), 85(2), 85(16), 85(19), 85(46), 85(49), 85(50), 86(40), 86(42), 86(47), 86(140), 87(146 octavo), 88(1 quarto), 89(235), 89(273), 93(*Brown's*), 93(*Claypoole's*), 93(*Dunlap's*), 93(*Gazette*), 93(*General Advertiser*), 93(*Porcupine's Gazette*)

RHODE ISLAND
Providence, 60(R.I. laws)

SOUTH CAROLINA
Charleston, 55(237)

VERMONT
Bennington, 60(Vt. laws)
Burlington, 35(379)
Rutland, 51(13), 60(Vt. laws)

Index to Dates of Publication

It was impossible to determine the specific date of publication for some titles in the 1812 catalogue. These entries are indexed as "after" the date of the first edition (e.g., after 1702) and are listed at the conclusion of this index.

1759, 12(383), 13(15), 18(51), 20(50), 37(85)
1760, 14(61), 88(76)
1761, 39(51), 52(250), 77(33)
1762, 22(28), 37(5), 61(Pa. laws)
1762–1807, 58(1 octavo)
1763, 16(58)
1763–87, 58(1 quarto)
1764, 27(199), 37(16)
1765, 22(19), 32(382), 61(Md. laws)
1766, 13(18)
1766–77, 79(5 folio)
1767, 21(16), 21(67), 68(9), 75(2), 78(39)
1768, 52(6), 29(25), 39(1)
1769, 55(212)
1769–73, 23(141)
1769–93, 48(8)
1770, 20(32), 32(505), 35(396), 50(118), 67(34), 86(45), 92(231)
1771, 24(43), 26(2 duodecimo), 56(90), 75(38), 78(9)
1772, 37(37), 47(53), 54(18), 69(1 folio), 75(1)
1773, 40(23), 41(14), 48(28)
1774, 18(416), 72(86), 72(92), 79(1)
1774–75, 22(21), 71(24)
1775, 23(93), 61(Pa. laws), 67(7), 71(47), 90(220)
1776, 32(381), 33(76), 36(91), 54(40), 56(15), 58(42), 60(N. J. laws), 90(39)
1776–81, 48(19)
1777, 15(454), 20 (3 quarto), 22(106)
1777–81, 39(Desbarre's)
1777–83, 88(59)
1778, 15(9), 29(28), 31(164), 33(51), 78(37), 87(50)
1778–79, 24(69)
1778–93, 14(62)
1779, 86(29)
1779–81, 34(159)
1779–84, 34(1 octavo)
1780, 34(161), 39(22), 56(26)
1780–87, 88(36)
1781, 12(10), 63(30)
1781–1801, 30(70), 30(85)
1782, 61(Pa. laws), 83(17)
1783, 19(502), 23(48), 64(1 quarto), 86(26)
1784, 15(374), 38(12), 38(17), 39(23), 49(104), 60(Conn. laws), 60(N.J. laws), 79(26)

1785, 30(389), 54(276), 64(2), 75(4 quarto), 75(4 Same), 81(5)
1785–89, 92(66)
1785–90, 54(241)
1785–96, 52(27)
1785–1800, 57(44)
1786, 14(147), 38(46), 40(55), 51(253), 86(31)
1787, 16(23), 22(386), 26(148), 27(399), 55(219), 57(108), 61(Md. laws), 74(53), 77(1)
1788, 12(283), 16(188), 20(412), 26(494), 30(446), 36(96), 60(252), 68(23), 76(97), 86(35)
1789, 19(13), 20(293), 38(86), 43(34), 50(3), 54(86), 60(N.Y. laws), 63(23), 66(55), 70(23), 87(58), 87(146 octavo), 89(207), 90(153)
1789–90, 17(645), 94(*Gazette*)
1790, 13(1), 16(274), 33(316), 36(33), 37(26), 44(95), 46(38), 51(58), 51(272), 51(282), 61(S.C. laws), 77(20), 82(1 quarto), 87(146 octavo), 91(37)
1790–94, 93(*General Advertiser*)
1790–99, 93(*Gazette*)
1791, 21(86), 24(81), 27(342), 29(30), 35(7), 39(14), 43(62), 53(245), 60(Vt. laws), 61(N.C. laws), 76(52)
1791–93, 52(244), 93(*Brown's*)
1791–94, 93(*Dunlap's*)
1791–95, 59(119)
1791–1801, 55(294)
1792, 19(74), 21(234), 25(422), 27(106), 28(41), 33(198), 41(2 quarto), 44(16 quarto), 52(180), 56(256), 57(214), 60(N.H. laws), 68(16), 70(22), 72(41), 74(71), 78(3 folio), 87(146 octavo), 89(273)
1792–94, 59(246)
1792–1809, 17(359)
1793, 18(83), 24(9), 24(70), 29(234), 35(157), 37(56), 40(1), 41(2 duodecimo), 51(13), 55(106), 59(93), 63(61), 64(1 octavo), 72(16), 75(40), 86(27), 90(37)
1793–94, 19(48)
1793–96, 69(1 octavo)
1793–1801, 61(Pa. laws)
1794, 21(270), 27(78), 28(37), 29(112), 31(62), 32(45), 35(151), 35(377), 41(3), 42(11), 42(117), 46(108),

1805–6, 29(299)

1805–7, 25(350)

1806, 17(306), 19(319), 20(257), 26(60), 31(334), 32(47), 35(64), 35(490), 40(105), 41(12), 42(5 duodecimo), 48(198), 51(61), 51(85), 52(184), 57(80), 58(235), 59(271), 60(N.Y. laws), 62(29), 63(18), 63(43), 64(12), 65(56), 66(30), 67(41), 69(18), 69(25), 69(29), 70(10), 71(59), 71(82), 73(15), 76(50), 76(66), 78(35), 79(9), 80(21), 83(18), 84(32), 84(34), 84(41), 85(15), 85(19), 86(20), 87(136), 89(339), 90(58), 90(119), 93(271)

1806–10, 93(*National Intelligencer*)

1807, 14(311), 15(335), 16(281), 20(340), 22(318), 24(260), 26(42), 26(443), 27(320), 30(406), 30(463), 38(13), 40(103), 44(15), 48(191), 50(263), 53(44), 53(46), 56(83), 58(264), 58(269), 62(13), 62(15), 62(55), 64(41), 68(13), 70(28), 71(90), 71(94), 74(96), 76(33), 79(14), 81(10), 83(19), 83(39), 84(29), 85(2), 85(42), 85(46), 85(49), 86(23), 86(39), 87(146), 87(163), 90(151), 90(174)

1808, 13(62), 13(503), 17(330), 19(Froissart's), 19(322), 22(46), 24(62), 25(428), 29(61), 36(19), 37(10 duodecimo), 38(4), 50(262), 53(195), 61(Va. laws), 62(52), 63(48), 64(40), 64(51), 65(46), 66(32), 67(57), 70(27), 71(34), 73(62), 73(66), 75(36), 80(15), 81(1 octavo), 81(8), 81(9), 82(1 octavo), 86(37), 86(60), 86(92), 89(326)

1808–10, 52(73)

1808–14, 82(2 folio)

1809, 23(61), 28(44), 35(379), 37(10 octavo), 42(81), 43(46), 49(67), 53(65), 55(237), 56(238), 71(35), 72(95), 77(77), 80(8), 81(7), 84(35), 86(40), 86(80), 87(158), 87(242), 89(235), 93(*Raleigh Star*)

1809–10, 34(326)

1809–13, 80(5)

1810, 14(248), 20(66), 23(486), 38(99), 42(9), 44(118), 45(70), 46(44), 51(236), 63(24), 63(26), 65(45), 65(50), 66(48), 68(26), 69(16), 80(7), 80(17), 82(37), 83(14), 84(25), 84(36), 87(160), 92(162)

1811, 15(385), 16(119), 17(504), 21(430), 39(84), 44(14), 48(107), 50(68), 51(58), 51(169), 53(51), 61(Lambert's), 61(Public Lands), 75(7), 81(1 octavo), 83(38), 86(36)

1812, 74(22), 80(14)

after 1702, 49(15)

after 1761, 92(1)

after 1778, 39(50)

after 1793, 83(15)

after 1795, 91(324)

after 1809, 18(11)

Title page, foreword, introduction, and index set by
FotoTypesetters, Inc. in ITC Garamond. Printed
and bound by Garamond/Pridemark Press,
Inc., of Baltimore on acid-free paper
manufactured by the S.D. Warren
Paper Company. Designed by
James E. Conner.